I0156986

The (Almost) Infinite Patience of God

THE (ALMOST) INFINITE PATIENCE OF GOD

JAMES KIFER

NEW HARBOR PRESS

RAPID CITY, SD

Copyright © 2017 by James Kifer

All rights reserved. No part of this publication may be reproduced, distributed or transmitted in any form or by any means, including photocopying, recording, or other electronic or mechanical methods, without the prior written permission of the publisher, except in the case of brief quotations embodied in critical reviews and certain other noncommercial uses permitted by copyright law. For permission requests, write to the publisher, addressed "Attention: Permissions Coordinator," at the address below.

Kifer/New Harbor Press
1601 Mt Rushmore Rd, Ste 3288
Rapid City, SD 57701
www.newharborpress.com

Ordering Information:
Quantity sales. Special discounts are available on quantity purchases by corporations, associations, and others. For details, contact the "Special Sales Department" at the address above.

The (Almost) Infinite Patience of God/ Kifer. -- 1st ed.
ISBN 978-1-63357-197-6

Contents

Preface

*I*t has long been called the "queen of virtues." This was an aphorism among both the ancient Greeks and of the Hebrews of the Bible, both Old and New Testaments. In a short phrase it encapsulates the importance of a quality which all but children, the habitually reckless and the grossly immature recognize in that to be successful in any endeavor patience must not only be present but a bedrock quality of one's efforts. It is patience, an attribute to which any sound thinking person aspires, and yet a virtue most persons regret not having in sufficient quantities.

Patience requires no scholarly treatise to prove its importance to us, for everyday in countless ways we witness its possession and demonstration as a requisite in almost all efforts, from the mighty to the seemingly mundane. We watch the remarkable patience of a young mother as she tenderly and lovingly copes with a decidedly impatient, thirsty and hungry infant. The stealthy patience of an ordinary domestic cat as he stalks his prey, real or imagined, captures our interested attention. In point of fact virtually all persons trundling about daily in their often overlooked, innocuous activities must exhibit more than a modicum of patience to get the tasks completed. Yet most of what we daily observe are examples of "short-term" patience, the patience of the moment or of the day and not necessarily the patience of which our ancient ancestors would have understood.

To our Biblical progenitors, the ancient Hebrews, patience was most likely and more properly understood as "endurance" or "to be long" and the record of Biblical stories comports well with this interpretation. The patience exhibited in ancient times and in these ancient accounts and records is often more akin to "longsuffering", a self-defining term which is itself often used as both a companion and a synonym for patience.

The early stories of the Bible are replete with patient longsuffering men and women. Abraham and Sarah waited past ordinary child-bearing ages to receive the promised blessing of a son, Isaac. That son with his wife Rebekah themselves waited many years before being honored with the blessing of twin boys. Much later the entire nation of the Israelites was forced to endure over four centuries of captivity and slavery before being liberated by their Deliverer. After later falling into slavery again the remnant of the Hebrew people, the nation of Judah, suffered several generations before being freed and returning to their homeland. Even today when studied and pondered these people and nations almost compel our awe and marveling at their moral, physical and spiritual endurance.

We may rightly praise all the above and this work seeks to examine the lives and stories of patience of many others. The foremost exemplar of patience, though, is God Himself, who in point of fact is regularly viewed not as supremely patient but rather as the opposite, supremely and even capriciously impatient. Regarding the quality of patience and God a belief, expounded, studied, and felt and propagated both explicitly and implicitly is so widely existent as to be pernicious. It is a tenet held by many that the Holy Bible is the account of not one, rather two Gods. The first God is the God of the Old Testament and He requires that His Creation grovel before Him. He is depicted as vengeful, quick to anger, lacking almost any semblance of patience and ferocious in His wrathful punishments. He orders the incineration of cities, the almost genocidal slaying of tribes and cultures and is quick to strike down in death even the leaders and priests of His own people. Any patience this God possess is mortgaged to His temper, which ultimately is destructive of earthly structures and of men and women. This, to many, is the God of the Old Testament. Yet, somehow as the last page of the Book of Malachi, the finale to the Old Testament, is turned He reappears as an entirely different God in the Gospel of Matthew, the introductory book of the New Testament.

This New Testament God has now become a Deity of love, possessed of limitless patience, sweet, gentle, and dare we say it, even a grandfatherly figure. This God removes Himself from center stage and now is seen in the person and character of His Son, Jesus Christ. This is the Great Physician, the Good Shepherd and the Prince of Peace. He calls all to Him and possesses abundant reservoirs of both patience and forgiveness. It is indeed a beautiful image and possessed of much truth. It certainly contrasts with the almost ugly image of the Old Testament God.

How can these two contradictory formulations and images of the same God be true? Some would aver that God's character has, in fact, changed through the ages. On the surface these summaries appear to be caricatures of two different entities. Yet if they are caricatures, they are caricatures believed in depth by multitudes of people, past, present and likely future. To the questions of whether these two images are reconcilable the plain answer is "No". Rather than attempt the impossible task of reconciliation the answer lies in a word employed in the previous sentence, the word being "images".

An image, of course, is a representation of something, be it a person, an object or even a fantasy, but it is not itself reality. God is too often viewed, now and in the past as well, as merely an image on which we project our perceptions of His reality. Too often the images are little grounded in truth or anything of substance, and most often reflect the image maker's preconceived notions of God. It is none too severe to state that the image of the Old Testament God is that of a tyrant until He radically alters Himself into an all forgiving Divinity that wants all to do right but quickly looks away, forgives and forgets any sin or crime, no matter how heinous. Again, neither Divine personage has any acquaintance with reality. The real God shown in both Testaments is immensely more engaging and interesting than these imaginary manifestations of human thinking. So how do we come to know this real God since no man or woman has ever seen Him? Here we could forward all sorts of propositions of the omnipresence of God, but we shall forego that route. The best source of information by far remains those same Testaments by which many label God as either "Old" or "New", but which they seldom read and upon which they perform little learned reflection. Hopefully these scriptures will reveal whether this God is a Father of patience and forgiveness or on the contrary, one of wrath and unshakeable vengeance. Fortunately, the Bible does more than merely proclaim God's character but also shows it through a plethora of interesting stories from both Testaments.

Likely the Old Testament group through which God was most revelatory of His character was the prophets, a noteworthy group of men so important that they, along with Christ's apostles, are referenced as the "foundation of the Church" itself. Through this assortment of men for century upon century God spoke His desires, His love, feelings, frustration and anger. A study of these men and their thoughts is more indicative of God's character than any other Biblical study, save the life of Christ Himself. To study them and understand theirs and God's character we will have to penetrate a fog of misunderstanding almost as great as that which engulfs God Himself.

If we concede that God has an "image" problem, we also must realize that it has been exacerbated by perceptions of the prophets, men who were often the voice of God on earth. As an agent is to his principal so were the prophets to God, being the almost literal embodiment of what the apostle Peter called the "oracles" of God. Although these men were as human as any who have ever lived most were highly cognizant of their roles and limitations and knew as Christ spoke long thereafter that real power and authority lay only with God. Almost all were extremely dutiful to their Divine charge, and most lived morally straight, even exemplary lives. It is not any creative imagination to state that most had a natural inclination to gentleness and a natural proclivity to mercy. They were, as much as it may be in a fallen world, the best and nearest representations of God found in the Old Testament. With the Heavenly Father they share another point of commonality. In their contemporary times and to this very moment in the twenty-first century, their nature and character has been abysmally portrayed and woefully slandered. The very term "Old Testament prophet" has in contemporary culture come to mean a wild-eyed fanatical, old man, living somewhere in seclusion in an ancient desert and springing forth occasionally to be a spiritual and cultural killjoy, stamping out the bright lights of enjoyment of the populace's well-deserved earthly pleasures. He is usually portrayed as unkempt, wearing animal skins, with a fiery haunted look in his eyes, somewhat akin to a modern meth addict. This repulsive person seeks to pronounce curses and death sentences upon all those who not immediately succumb to the Divine Will. In short, he is to both modern and even Biblical eyes an entirely loathsome person to which no sane, sentient being would want any contact. If this is God's oracle, the symbol of the Divine person, we want nothing to do with such an impatient and vindictive God and His crazed prophets. These images contain hints and a tincture of reality, but in the main they comprise a wildly inaccurate and misstated portrayal of God and His messengers.

A closer reading and study of the lives and stories of these oft-slandered men will uncover many truths, in actuality that while they were heralds of God and necessarily at times plain speaking, they are more readily to be seen as the heralds of God's almost limitless patience. Rather than hurling fiery missiles of fire and righteous indignation these prophets are more readily viewed as pleading, begging, entreating and coaxing the nations of Israel and Judah and finally all of humanity to abandon paganism and follow the one true God of love. These supposedly "hardened", and "hard-hearted" men frequently wept over the condition of nations and people they genuinely loved. As hopefully this work will demonstrate their harshest words were reserved usually for priests, various religious officials, princes and kings and in generally the proud and the vain.

To many still, though, in the modern age of which we live, an epoch in which vast multitudes have no perception and no religious training whatsoever any old prophet is a curiosity, a weird representation of a bygone age best forgotten. They are distasteful specters from a distant and remote past, embarrassments to an age of sophisticates which has escaped such hocus-pocus and superstition. Our current era mis-defines humanism and makes men and women the measure of all things. To many establishment minds and avant-garde thinkers those who dissent from the modern consensus of thought are pathetic and pitiable forms. To acknowledge wisdom and value in the prophets is to validate ancient rituals and nonsense. Remarkably, whether known to them or not, the modern reaction to the prophets and their Divine messages is precisely that of the non-believer three millennia past in the Old Testament. Bluntly stated the historic exchange between King Ahab and Elijah remains prescient:

> "...Ahab said unto (Elijah), Art thou that troubleth Israel. And (Elijah) answered, I have not troubled Israel, but thou..."

The fury of God was shown on very limited occasions by the prophets. Far more often, though, did God demonstrate through these noteworthy men a patience which is grand, unexplainable and awe inspiring. It was a patience that would test and drive any human beyond human limits. It was/is a patience that is the sole property of the Creator of the universe. But what of these men who were the prophets, who were so vital to God's eternal plans? Do they bear a resemblance to the perceptions and caricatures of both the moderns and the ancients? Only in very incidental and tangential manner would the answer be in the affirmative. The base answer to such a question is resoundingly no, and a brief study of the prophets reveals not Divine fury but Divine patience.

In our times we praise a god which has been created by man himself, and that god answers to the familiar name of "Diversity". The original author of diversity was God Himself. Although all the men on whom the spotlight shall be shined are Hebrew, Israelite or Jewish (the names according with the times in which they lived) race and nationality measures little with God. We will look upon the likes of Moses, living in wealth and comfort from childhood, to his rise as perhaps the major spiritual figure before Christ Himself. The prophets had among their number men who were extremely well trained and highly educated, names such as Samuel, Isaiah and Daniel coming to the fore. The humblest in the person of Amos are represented, as are the wealthy in a man such as Elisha. Reluctance, fierce obstinate reluctance is found in the persons of Jeremiah and even perhaps, especially in Moses. Likely, the two men most known and studied as prophets are Elijah and John the Baptist, and each superficially comes nearer in their approach to the cliched image of prophets then any others. Yet closer scrutiny may compel a different conclusion.

Their characters and personalities seem to have been as varied and differentiated as any other group of people at any time; however, they did have some consistencies which bound them together. Many of them tested and tried the patience of God Himself. In moments of fear, depression and anger they could be petulant, impatient (sometimes with God) and in many instances not really the most enthusiastic participants in the roles assigned to them by God. As often (not very) that they displayed impatience towards the multitudes to whom they were directed to prophecy they more readily and more often demonstrated impatience towards God. For those wishing to see the stereotypical "Hollywood" portrayal of the prophets as the fierce avengers and the hands of God's wrath disappointment awaits. This standard portrayal casts the typical prophet in the part of an old, bitter curmudgeon who drapes crepe upon every scene and upon every person. He finds sinners under every stone and is almost giddily eager to punish transgressors.

To many, then and now thousands of years hence they were opprobrious wizened old men, and simultaneously objects of fun and ridicule. They were judgmental, harsh and hateful and the very antitheses to the "spirit of the times". Let us be honest, for throughout the ages for the vast multitudes of both believers and non-believers as much as any human can be, they were the human image of God.

It has become an axiomatic statement that "God is Love", yet God is much more than love. Maybe, though, we could define our definition of God to love, if but for discussion, since love is a jeweled diamond of many facets. As we began this Introduction, we recall that patience is the centerpiece of all facets, and from this virtue much of the character of God radiates. The Bible is among other matters a veritable compendium of patience, shown through the lives and words of His prophets and ultimately demonstrated through His son, Jesus Christ.

All have taxed and tried the patience of many, especially those who are loved the deepest and dearest. Before the light of day is even seen by infant eyes for nine months or so we have already taxed the patience of our mothers. Regardless of anyone's life story he or she has challenged the patience of a wide and vast array of persons. The author of these essays claims no exception and wishes to sincerely thank all who have exhibited patience to him a patience which in some instances has made almost Divine demands upon its exhibitors. Foremost are all that have given me such love and joy in life, commencing with my beloved mother and father, the very exemplars of parental patience. My daughters, grandchildren and assorted family members deserve plaudits for demonstrating more than a modicum of patience. In this life and above all I must thank and pay tribute to the abiding and endearing patience of my treasured wife, Debbie, with whom we have made our marriage of almost five decades the centerpiece of our lives.

Still, one other person who I never met and whose name I do not know must be the subject of a tribute. It was perhaps twenty-five years ago that one morning I was scanning the obituaries in the local newspaper. One woman's obituary was not lacking the standard information and life statistics, but it also included a statement she herself had written. Although this is likely not an exact quotation, she left the following message to be absorbed and remembered to her children:

"Learn to forgive each other, for we all need a lot of forgiveness in our lives."

Surely this gracious lady would not object to our adding "patience" to forgiveness.

Chapter 1

MOSES: I LED THREE LIVES

*F*or seemingly endless ages Egypt was the recognized political, cultural and intellectual center of the ancient world. Commencing in the third millennium B.C. Egypt slowly but surely and meticulously developed a civilization of such culture, depth and spectacle that it remains a center of study even into the twenty-first century AD. It was a culture the influence of which is by no means fully exhausted even today. Many major universities throughout the world maintain separate studies on Egypt, and scholars famous in their own realm continue to expand our knowledge of ancient Egypt through the academic discipline of Egyptology.

In some degree the Egyptians began to coalesce politically around 3,000 B.C., and it is likely that within three centuries hence the structures for which Egypt is most famous, the pyramids and particularly the great pyramids at Giza were built, the sole representation of the Seven Wonders of the World still standing. These visually imposing and fascinating structures remain the very symbol of Egypt in the eyes of the world. They have cast such a huge and permanent shadow that much of the Egyptian culture and heritage has been seemingly dimmed. How unfortunate this has proven to the common human understanding.

The Egyptians were creators, organizers and builders, so just who were these remarkable persons? The origins of the Egyptian people remain a continuing topic of debate among scholars, but for our purposes suffice it to say that they considered themselves a unique, distinct people. For the ancient world they were fairly tall, perhaps 5" 6" for men and five feet for women, with strong but fine features. Except for certain social castes and in contrast to most other ancient peoples, the men were smooth shaven, and even in a desert climate placed an emphasis on personal hygiene.

It was not the pyramids alone for which the Egyptians were famous builders. They built great temples, obelisks, various memorials and still extant structures, most with slave or conscripted labor. In literature, music and art they surpassed their contemporaries in the ancient world. Along with the Hebrews but drawing far different lessons and conclusions they were among the first to seriously study humanity's relationship to the Divine.

The Divine employed the land, culture and politics of ancient Egypt in matters and to an extent surpassed by no other nation, other than the chosen Israel itself. The patience of God played upon the stage and theater of this ancient empire to a breathtaking extent, and it all began with something universally declaimed as bad - a famine – Circa 1900-1800 B.C. the adjacent small land of Canaan was in the throes of a deadly famine. To gather grain and sustenance the Biblical patriarch Jacob dispatched ten of his remaining eleven sons to Egypt on a mission literally of life and death. Another son, Joseph, was presumed dead, but in an extraordinary series of events this remarkable young man had proceeded them to Egypt, effectively becoming, after the King, himself, the nation's foremost ruler and authority. An oft-told story as intense and emotional as any in history unfolded, and the children of Jacob (a/k/a Israel) migrated to

Egypt where they became honored and welcomed guests. They were esteemed, they grew in numbers and prosperity until the day, the Book of Exodus recorded:

"(T)here arose up a new king over Egypt, who knew not Joseph."

Now, the Hebrews, longtime guests and neighbors, were enslaved by the Egyptians, who enchained them to "hard bondage", and bitter, rigorous slavery. Yet the Hebrew population grew to such a level that the King decreed the death of all Hebrew boy babies, thus foreshadowing Herod's "Slaughter of the Innocents" in the New Testament. The King has his way, but more so did God.

The events and even spectacles which comprise the core, the creative heart of the Old Testament now begin to make their appearances, and among other matters the patience of God in its depth, promise, suffering and finally its limitation play their roles. It all begins with a very small baby floating in a basket upon the greatest of rivers.

A. Moses, the Egyptian

The baby was born to two Hebrews of the tribe of Levi, Amram and Jochebed. Jochebed, the mother, recognized that her baby was born dead unless she could affect its rescue. With the ingenuity of a desperate mother she placed the baby in a well-prepared basket and placed the basket in the river's banks where the King's daughter and friends were bathing. The royal princess discovered the basketed baby and adopted it for her own, sending for the baby's mother to nurse him. They baby, now given the name Moses, becomes the world's most important single man before Christ, the Biblically described greatest leader of men ever known and a man whose influence is of monumental proportions even today. Yet the baby Moses is at the center of one of history's greatest ironies. Daily, the King's servants and soldiers are sent forth, and daily they wipe from their swords and daggers the blood of newly born Hebrew babies. Aside from the grotesque immorality of this holocaust there remains a truth that cannot be denied. The Egyptian King, the Pharaoh as we know him, was slaughtering babies with abandon. He only needed to kill one, and that one was Moses, whom he was raising and nurturing in his own household.

To discern who, what and why Moses became the towering spiritual and historical figure we must commence an examination of his early years. Unfortunately, though, we are given but little material to peruse. The written historical accounts of the young Moses are limited to the Bible, and particularly the second chapter of Exodus. Here begins a long earthly tenure which for study is readily divided into three phases. The patience of Moses is prominent, but it is the patience of God which is paramount. The lifespan of Moses alone, when fully studied, tells a diligent student all that needs to be known not just of Moses, but of God's patience, a patience that is Divinely profound and that snaps once or twice.

First, though, what of Moses, the child, the growing youth and the burgeoning young man in his prime? Moses, as most well-known figures, is two persons, the perceived and the reality. No where is this more true than with this great deliverer. Artistically, Moses is one of the most honored persons in history, perhaps culminating in Michelangelo's magnificent statue. A centerpiece of the Old Testament he is referenced another 79 times in the New Testament. Yet to multitudes of a certain age he is inextricably linked with an actor's portrayal in the 1956 motion picture, "The Ten Commandments". Succinctly stated, to generations the famous actor Charlton Heston is Moses. Although the faith and determination of Moses is well captured by Mr. Heston, his Moses is one of overwhelming, even intimidating, power, whereas the scriptures term him "the meekest of men". Meek, though, he was and silent as are the scriptures we may infer that Moses lacked nothing as he grew and matured as Pharaoh's daughter, Hebrew by birth and heritage and Egyptian be training. For the upper class (and does it get more elevated than Pharaoh's household) the Egyptians provided education through scholars and tutors. Doubtless much was expected of Moses, and his life's story shows that he answered those expectations.

One day while among his fellow Hebrews he witnessed an Egyptian physically attacking and abusing a slave. With surrepetition Moses killed the Egyptian, and whether he had moral justification we may only offer conjecture, for the Bible remains silent. For Moses, though, he found the next day that his presumed clandestine killing was the subject of witnesses. He intervened in a fight between two Hebrews, and the aggressor of the two hurled into Moses face the barbed comment that no one man made you a judge over us and venomously asked Moses if he intended to kill them, as he had the Egyptian. Now, Moses being high placed in the social order drew the eye of Pharaoh himself, who sought to kill Moses.

After fleeing across an expanse of desert he arrived in Midian at a well at which he drove away shepherds who had bullied past the seven daughters of Jethro. To these daughters Moses was an Egyptian and so they identified him to their father. Moses ad Jethro evidently shared a mutual respect, and it was soon bound by his marriage to Jethro's daughter, Zipporah. So ended the first phase of the life of Moses, and the "Egyptian" passed into historical memory.

B. Moses, the Shepherd

Now begins that period in the life of Moses far away from the intense glare of the spotlight and of history, in which he settles into a successful occupation and presumed domestic tranquility, for with his wife Zipporah he has two sons, Gersham and Eleazar. Far from the groans of toil, bondage and poverty by which his fellow Hebrews endure lives of misery and degradation, Moses's life has entered a period of respite, of learning and of patience. Yet, the patience of another has come to a juncture in time, and the Divine longsuffering is about to give way to action. The great enslaving Pharaoh dies "in the process of time," and the agonizing cry of His people rises to God, who remains fully aware of the old covenant which He had made with the great patriarchs, Abraham, Isaac and Jacob – the covenant, that their descendants would become a great nation and through them all the people of the world would be blessed. But in slavery? God's patience bore four centuries of witnessing the debasement of his own, but this term was about to expire, for God had been patiently preparing and tutoring a great Deliverer.

But what of Moses during this protracted middle segment of his life? When last viewed he had been a cultured, well educated privileged killer (whether justified or not), a fugitive from the unconquerable wrath of the most powerful man on earth, the Egyptian Pharaoh. Moses had been transformed into the humble role of a shepherd, an important but common occupation in the times of the ancients, but hardly one gilded with glamor or presumably a training ground for national and world leadership. Yet for such a humble trade its role of Biblical notables is long and significant. Later we find David, likely Israel's greatest political and military figure, commencing hos journey to fame as a shepherd boy. Many of the prophets which will be observed were shepherds, and the first to see Christ in Bethlehem's manager were humble shepherds. Naturally, this culminates in a recognition that the Savior Himself is the Good Shepherd.

Tending sheep offers a lifetimes symposium in patience, for sheep, as all livestock and even our domestic dogs and cats are not easily regimented. Nor are they particularly intelligent, possessing a will to do what they desire and at the time of their choosing. Constant care and attention must be expended and lavished upon them all especially the renegades, the obstinate and the ill. To the shepherd they are invaluable, and to the good shepherd a source and subject of his vigilant care, nurturing and love. Sheep tend to stray, and a flock demands the constant attention of the shepherd, whose job can never be temporary, part-time or even confined to a forty-hour span within one week. As any trade, business, occupation, profession or "job" by any nomenclature it requires learning over an extended period of time. Remarkably, sheep and humans bear more than a superficial resemblance, and the comparison of shepherding sheep with managing a nation is no flippancy.

Moses, already a supremely gifted and blessed man with open doorways into both the Egyptian and Hebrew cultures was given a calm, quiet, though highly important regimen of training in this mid-life period of exile and isolation. He doubtless employed it wisely, for eventually he literally saw the burning light which would begin an epoch and accelerate God's plan of redemption for humanity.

On what was likely an otherwise ordinary day Moses led his flock to the base of Mount Horeb where his eye caught the sight of a burning bush on the mountain, a bush engulfed in a flame which would not be extinguished. He "turned aside" to see this strange sight and God spoke to him from the fire, introducing himself as the God of the patriarchs and His desire to deliver His people from the slavery of Pharaoh and his minions. This deliverance would not be the personal appearance of God or His angels but by the hand and leadership of one chosen man, and that man was Moses. Was he ready for the responsibility? To this question Moses gave not the answer "No" but a seemingly endless series of "Not me!" God's appearance to Moses at the Burning Bush and the lengthy dialogue with Moses becomes a template, an exemplar, a microcosm, of His "almost" endless patience with humanity. Most assuredly Moses now stretches God's patience taut, but we must conduct self-examinations, look into our hearts and ask the questions "Can we really blame Moses" and know that doubtless we would each do the same, or worse. Moses is assigned by God the most difficult mission in man's history, one from which almost all but the most deluded individuals would recoil. He, a shepherd, is to return to Egypt and demand from Pharaoh, the single most powerful man on earth, the release and emancipation of a nation on whom for some four centuries the Egyptians have been extremely dependent for labor. Further, unknown now by all but a few, he is to present himself to his own people, the Israelites, as their leader and deliverer. Then his charge is to lead this mass of humanity from slavery across a desert and to Mount Sinai to worship a God, whose very name is unknown to them.

Moses excites our respect and perhaps admiration for the litany of reasoned excuses he now lays before God. Initially, he proclaims with sound sense that no one, be they Egyptian or Hebrew, has any reason to listen to me, a stranger to them. The Lord patiently answers Moses with a display of His miraculous powers and assures him that while in Egypt he will be able to call upon God for displays of signs and wonders. God's assurance is a reminder that he will not be a totally free agent and that the Divine will work His will through a man, Moses.

The mental agility of Moses is wielded by him with the quickness of a rapier, and he offers to God a reason that to this day is employed countlessly by men and women who are given speaking, especially public, speaking assignments, that being that "I am not eloquent." God in the tender manner of a patient, loving Father by no means scoffs at or brushes aside this objection. Yes, Moses excuses continue unabated, and finally God's anger begins to be piqued, and He declaims that Moses's brother, Aaron, a polished speaker will accompany Moses in his endeavors against Pharaoh. As if God's presence alone was not sufficient for Moses, the inclusion of his brother in his company seems to assuage him. So, Moses, already having pushed God's patience returns to Egypt, so ending the second of his three lives.

C. Deliverer, Lawgiver and Prophet

Upon returning to Egypt, Moses is joined by his elder brother Aaron, and they meet with the elders of Israel for a "briefing" and the announcement of impending freedom. As with many of our fears one of Moses proves unfounded because the Hebrew people accepted Moses as God's messenger, their deliverer and leader. Only now would events transpire and result in a confrontation which would test the nettle and patience of all parties.

Two Levite brothers, one a complete unknown and the other a "has-been" secure an audience with the single greatest power on earth, Pharaoh, a man proclaimed and worshipped by his people as a god. No army, no man or woman, no civilization nor culture can conceivably challenge his unquestioned power and sovereignty. Yet, here he has before him what must seem a pathetic joke, a demand by two nobodies representing an unknown God to free a nation which for almost half a millennium has been an invaluable resource to the Egyptian throne and people. It is impossible to overstress the importance of the sequence of events which now begin, and it is equally futile to deny the white-hot emotions which they generate among the participants. As to patience Pharaoh's is non-existent, for he issues an edict that not only will the Hebrews remain slaves but that the bricks which they daily construct to feed the Pharaoh's voracious appetite for construction but that these bricks will be made without the superstructure of straw.

Not for the last time is Moses now entrapped in a vice of impatience, with Pharaoh's oppression crushing the Israelites even more, but now with Moses's own fellow Hebrews blaming not Pharaoh, but Moses and Aaron for attracting greater burdens to them. Also, not for the final time does God demonstrate that His patience is greater than others. The great contest between two kings, a Pharaoh of unchallengeable earthly power and the King of the Universe, who dispatches Moses to Pharaoh to determine who is really God in Egypt. Nine elements of pure horror now rain down upon Pharaoh and his dominion, which coupled with a finale we know as the Ten Plagues. To coerce Pharaoh into liberating the slaves such terrors as water turning to blood, flies, locusts, darkness and others make a visitation upon the great Egyptians, and nine times do all the actions play from the same script. At first Pharaoh, repulsed by each horror, agrees to free the Hebrews, and then repents of his decision to emancipate the Hebrews. Each time, while God's patience is sorely tried, He answers with another plague, and the cycle begins anew. This fiery "vengeful and wrathful" deity of Old Testament lore has waited over four centuries to free His chosen people so He can abide Pharaoh's vacillations a bit longer. Yet to prod the mighty ruler He sends the tenth plague, the death of all firstborn children, be they man or beast, in Egypt. Only the obedient Israelites who have marked their doors with the blood of lambs are passed over from the terrors of the calamity. Now, Pharaoh's will is bent to Moses and to God, for Pharaoh wakens to find his own eldest son dead. The exodus from Egypt, an event long promised, but for which God bided His time patiently for hundreds of years is on the brink of its appearance until one day it comes. Perhaps over a million Hebrews are led by Moses away from the degrading slavery of Egypt and into the uplands of law and freedom. It may be cogently and forcefully argued, though, that no nation, no single group of people has ever tried the patience of God (and Moses) more than this generation of Israelites. As this multitude happily and even gleefully exited Exodus to accurately reflect their hearts and spirits they should have been carrying banners addressed to God, reading 'What have you done for me lately?' For it is a generation which will literally destroy itself with childish petulance, self-will and a complete lack of patience.

At the literal and precise sight of the most famous of Old Testament miracles the Israelites, slaves for generations, reveal their hand. Pharaoh, a man of changing intentions and vacillating desires, has changed his mind and decided that the descendants of Joseph would not be free after all, and with his mobile force overtook the Israelites at the edge of the Red Sea. Immediately upon the sight of the Egyptians the Hebrews quaked with fear and anger at Moses, lamenting their presumed fate and exclaiming:

"For it had been better for us to serve the Egyptians, than that we should die in the wilderness."

After performing the seemingly impossible task of liberating a nation of slaves the immediacy of the nation's hurling its insults and impatience must have been startling to even God himself. As even every child knows (or once knew) through Moses God parts the waters, enabling the Hebrew escape and crashes them together, thereafter, drowning and destroying the Pharaoh's army. For a brief moment of triumph and exultation the Israelites were on the shining path for

"...the people feared the Lord, and believed the Lord, and His servant Moses."

A word must be spoken of the character of the Israelites, but the word is applicable to Israelite, Egyptian, any nationality or race, ancient or modern and is the recognition of a human condition. The people which Moses freed from Egypt were slaves, and the slavery extended its dark roots deeply into the past. Neither they, nor their parents, grandparents or anyone within memory knew anything but bondage. They had been horribly abused, as are most slaves, but slaves nonetheless they were, and with the stunted maturity and mentality of slaves. They knew how to work, how to obey and how to be servile to demanding taskmasters. This generation was unacquainted with the demands and responsibilities of freedom, just as children are innocent of the burdens of reasoned thinking and decision making. And it most certainly showed in almost every conceivable fashion and situation.

After the wonder and grandeur of the miracles and their own rescue had worn away the Israelites began to complain that their wandering in the wilderness was driving them to starvation, and that they were dying of thirst. Again, God miraculously provided both water and the yet renown "manna from heaven" for their nourishment.

Although now in no danger of death they soon tired of the supposed blandness of the manna and issued new complaints, further stretching the patience of both Moses and especially God.

Still, finally came the day that was the proclaimed and announced purpose for the exodus. The Israelites had crossed the Sinai Desert and made camp at the base of the mountain of God, Mont Sinai itself. Now comes the oft told and frequently depicted story of God's summoning of Moses to the mount, His conversation and the dispensation of The Law and known more succinctly as "The Ten Commandments", the basis of the Jewish and then the Christian moral systems and, in truth, the ethical foundation of a civilized society. Oh, but how long has everybody waited! Moses has lived enough life for several men, striding the worlds of Egyptian and Hebrew, freedom and slave, an outcast, a fugitive, a humble shepherd and now the primary Divine instrument for the establishment of a nation and not just a legal system but "The Law" itself. He has patiently lived in exile, overcome the fear of confronting the all-powerful Pharaoh and has freed literally an entire nation. He is rewarded by being in the presence of God himself and receiving the codified basis of morality directly from the Almighty.

The patience of God is beyond that of Moses, great though his was, and it existed at a Divine level which mankind cannot attain. Through Creation itself, the Fall of Man and the great epic stories of Genesis God had patiently brought His people to Egypt. In His wisdom, though, He knew it was not yet time, so over four centuries elapsed before He had the conditions He desired, the conditions and the man, Moses. Already He has confronted the reluctance of Moses, the obstinacy of Pharaoh and the almost infantile behavior of the Israelites, and He remained abiding and patient and fulfilled His purposes.

Patience is a virtue of the mature, and its opposite impatience is the province of the child. Moses tarried on Mount Sinai longer than the people thought necessary (as if they had a repository of similar events upon which to come to this judgment), became restless and decided that this "crisis" of Moses absence was too great an opportunity to bypass. With an insouciant heart they merged three desires into one, the first being the abandonment of God for the worship of a golden calf, foolishly and inexplicably fashioned by Aaron. The golden calf, though, was not to be a one-time stationary object but was to be taken before them as they returned to Egypt, a "living" symbol that they had physically and emotionally returned to paganism, from which the hearts of many Hebrews likely had never left. Finally, many of the Hebrews, with Moses's absence, just wanted to have fun.

What a patient God was the deity which the Hebrews worshipped, the same God we worship today. Yet the patience, while it is almost infinite to those whom He loves, the key operative word is "almost". It can be and here it was exhausted. Both Testaments demonstrate a God who will abide and tolerate difficulties and travails longer than will any of His creation. Although He doubtless is not pleased with His disciples He will tolerate (for a season or two) laziness, obstinance, reluctance, lack of enthusiasm, whining, complaining and an almost endless roster of wrongs. He now establishes dramatically that there is existent one conduct which is intolerable, and that is rebellion.

God's wrath was not satisfied by a mere chastisement but rather He had three thousand Hebrews slain, and likely would have killed more save for the intercession of Moses. A modicum of time, though, had been required for Moses's own anger to subside. Earlier after descending from Sinai in rage he broke the stone tablets of the law, then ordered the golden calf pulverized into powder which was mixed into the water supply and which the Israelites were now forced to drink. The tumult eventually calmed, and after approximately one year at Sinai Moses led the Israelites on the presumed path to Canaan, the Promised Land. The nation came to a place called Kadesh, which was effectively to be the Israelite base of operations for the conquest of Canaan. As a good commander Moses dispatched spies, or scouts, into Canaan on a reconnaissance mission to determine what awaited them. Twelve men, one from each Hebrew tribe, were selected, and they made a forty-day tour of Canaan before returning. Ten were unanimous that the Israelite cause was hopeless and that the Canaanites were simply too numerous and powerful. Only two, Joshua and Caleb, were confident that they could fulfill God's prophecy and take the land.

All this was finally enough for the Israelite people, and they erupted into open insurrection against Moses and Aaron, planning to choose new leadership and return to Egypt, slinking back like the slaves there were. They planned to stone to death Moses and Aaron and be free of their God once and for all-time. this same God, though, described as "...merciful, gracious, and longsuffering..." had been tried long enough. His patience, extended beyond the limitations of endurance of any mortal man, the cup of His exasperation running over, the Lord of Hosts finally broke with these people. Their punishment was a denial of the promises own fulfillment and death. With the exception of the loyal and far-sighted Joshua and Caleb all the generations over twenty years of age which had been miraculously extracted from Egypt would perish in the desert, after the peoples' famed forty years wandering in the wilderness.

So now Moses continued to bear the burdens of leadership for a nation that literally was going nowhere. Forty years is a long time, but eventually that troublesome, querulous and childish people who had left the dismal slavery of Egypt died. In its place had arisen a new nation of Israel, a people that though they too were flawed, had been hardened by four decades of rough living and were toughened physically, emotionally and spiritually of fulfilling the covenant to take the land of Canaan. They had the means, the desire, the opportunity, and the leader, but that leader was not to be Moses.

In those memorable words at the conclusion of the Pentateuch, though Moses was now old

"...his eye was not dim, nor his natural force abated."

The God of infinite patience had found in the Hebrew/Egyptian a man who drew upon a vast reservoir of patience for a very long time. He had performed magnificently in every conceivable situation, upon every stage and with so many exasperating persons, but was Moses the man to lead the Israelites in a brutal military campaign in Canaan. God had a brilliant leader for this task, but his name was not Moses, but Joshua.

Yet this demands from us the query of "Why not Moses?" While he was the greatest of leaders, he was not the perfect leader. Earlier, in their wanderings Moses, exasperated by his people's behavior disobeyed God in a famous incident wherein water was miraculously provided Israel in the desert. Although God still let the waters flow, He advised Moses that his penalty would be denial of entrance into Canaan. A severe penalty it undoubtedly was, but it likely illustrated God's insistence that no man or woman was above the law. It is ours to conjecture if perhaps there were other Divine reasons for the denial of Moses's entrance into Canaan. As the scriptures are about to unfold, we see that Israel would be engaged in a long, arduous and even savage military campaign against the Canaanites, who themselves were hardly pushovers. Perhaps God realized that this was a burden best carried by a younger man, and he had such in Joshua. Also, He is in advance of our human realization that while a person may be exemplary, even brilliant in one or more roles, it does not follow that he will be exemplary in all. Joshua, not Moses, was the man of the hour.

What do we say of the patience of God throughout the "lives" of Moses? Truly, only the word Divine comes close to adequacy as a descriptive term. God literally had to confront "The Good, the Bad and the Ugly." The "Bad" was a role which had many actors, foremost among them Pharaoh and later an Israelite insurrection helmed by Korah. "Ugly" is the proper nomenclature for the seemingly endemic childish petulance and evil of the Israelite people, which God bore with a patience several rungs above the human. Finally, yes, He had to contend with the "Good" in Moses, a man who possessed in accompaniment with all his superlative traits a temper and a limit to his patience. The Lord of Hosts contended all this and eventually accomplished His purpose of placing His chosen people in the Promised Land. His eternal plan of humanity's redemption would not be thwarted.

Moses? After viewing in panoramic splendor Canaan from afar he died and was buried on Mount Nebo. In an oft quoted line from Shakespeare young Prince Hamlet says of his treacherously murdered father:

"Take him all in all we shall not see his like again."

As great as was the poet the Bible's epitaph for Moses was greater still:

"And there arose not a prophet since in Israel, like unto Moses, whom the Lord knew face to face."

Chapter 2

HAVE IT YOUR WAY: THE REJECTION OF SAMUEL

*J*srael's conquest of Canaan was a long and arduous and at times spectacular and glorious but always deep in blood and gore. The united twelve tribes were blessed with a dedicated, experienced and talented general and leader in Joshua and were successful in subduing most, but not all, of Canaan, as excitely related in the Book of Joshua. In this period God too received the benefit of a blessing in that he could rely upon a leader and servant in the person of Joshua who was just as dedicated as Moses. The Israelites themselves were not the erstwhile abject slaves of Egypt but now were hardened by forty years in tough desert conditions, and hardened they needed to be.

The conquest of Canaan has run afoul of the guardians of modern political sensibilities and has been labeled an aggressive unprovoked war against a people, the Canaanites, who had not levied war upon Israel. It has been condemned and excoriated as malicious and spiteful, a stain on the reputation of God Himself. Through modern (and to an extent, ancient) eyes there is found a bedrock of truth in these allegations. Militarily and politically Israel was unprovoked, and as with all wars the results were sanguinary in the extreme. God required Israel to conquer the Canaanites before the Canaanites conquered them. Not necessarily in the military sense (though that was certainly likely) but in the moral and spiritual sphere. In many ways this eventually occurred, and God knew the potency and temptation of the Canaanite system and lifestyle, a regimen of hedonism and immorality to which the major part of Israel eventually succumbed.

Joshua, too, went the way of all flesh, and Israel required new leadership. At this juncture, however, God had no person of the stature of Joshua ready to succeed Moses. The Israelites were in Canaan, but the Canaanites were not pacified, and in fact retained an aggressive spirit on at least two fronts. The first is the traditional military arena where the Israelites began to suffer defeats, and the second, the one with more lasting consequences, was the moral. The system of Baal worship, so identified with Canaan, began to penetrate the Hebrew mind and conscience and remained a spiritually acidic presence for another thousand years. It destroyed most of Israel with only the famous "remnant" being saved. Yet, for now, God needed new leadership and in many respects a new governmental system.

For this He commenced an extended period wherein Israel would be ruled by Judges, but in actuality God sought to rule Israel Himself through these judges. In the language of modern political science Israel would be a "theocracy". The selection of a man named Othniel inaugurated this period, a tenure which ended with the most famous of judges, Samuel. Thirteen men and one woman served as judges, some whose conduct was deplorable, others as historical non-entities, but four in particular stand high in accomplishment and fame. The four, around whom attention still coalesces are Deborah, Gideon, Samson and above all, Samuel, likely as great a man as found in the Old Testament.

Still, the period of the Judges was in no sense a time of tranquility. Paganism and its corruptive and corrosive effects began to nibble first at the edges of the nation and finally at its heart. It was a time of ceaseless warfare, first with the Canaanites and later with such as the Midianites and most importantly, the Philistines. Battles were fought, battles were won, and battles were lost, and the Israelites grew fearful and weary of war. God grew weary of the Israelites, but He did not desert them, and many of the most famous names and events in their history begin to unfold.

Israel's first great judge was not a man, but rather a woman, Deborah. A very wise woman aided by a fine general, Deborah directed the outnumbered Israelites to a victory over the technologically more advanced Canaanites in the plain of Esdraelon, a victory which Deborah commemorated with history's first known narrative epic poem.

Still, the Israelites faltered, and their foes were generally stronger and uncompromising. The Hebrew nation remained sporadic in their obedience, and the idolatry of Israel and its enemies' strength and determined resiliency remained obdurate. Esdraelon, unlike many of history's battles, brought a general peace for forty years. Deborah passed from the scene, and Israel was confronted by a huge eastern invasion from the Midianites and Amalekites, both ancient enemies and now entirely successful in reducing Israel's economy to a shambles. They invaded at harvest time, and Israel was seemingly at the mercy of these foreigners, their economy wrecked and their military a shadow of its enemies' forces. Not for the last time did God raise up a man who was suited to a dire situation, a man named Gideon who became both judge and general. Commencing with an army of 22,000 the Lord had Gideon gradually winnow his forces to only 300, a proverbial "few good men" who were willing to give all in fighting the hosts of Midian. Miraculously, God granted the 300 a victory, and the Israelites glorified not God, but Gideon. Gideon was an enigmatic figure, but apparently possessed a great personal attraction and magnetism, and to him many Israelites wished to give a crown as their king. Again, God's patience must have been burnt close to its end, for it was God through Gideon who won the great triumph. Nonetheless, Gideon remained in office, but as judge not as king, and most importantly the land and nation were accorded another forty years of rest and peace.

Winds, gale force, violent winds began to blow from the southwest, as Israel's most tenacious, famous and enduring enemy began its ascent to regional power. It was Philistia, the land of the Philistines, who would not be conquered in a day. In Israel over the ensuing decades the sad cycle of history drearily repeated itself – the lapse into paganism, the fear of enemies which would prostrate Israel before God, imploring salvation, God's deliverance of the nation and a relapse into idolatry. A number of judges came and went, none of particular notoriety, until finally the office was opened to a man from the tribe of Dan, a man who became, with David, one of the two great men of "glamour" in the Old Testament. He was Samson, of prodigious strength and dare we employ that slippery term "charisma", a man who has likely been the subject to as many tales, motion pictures, television dramas and artistic depictions as any in the Old Testament. Legendary for his strength, power and virility neither then nor today does he easily accommodate the image of judicial sobriety. Still, he served God until his great fatal weakness, beautiful women, robbed him of his dignity, his hair and eyesight. In death, though, Samson redeemed himself in the eyes of history by literally "bringing down the house," destroying their temple and a large swath of the Philistine aristocracy.

Still, nothing of earthly or heavenly consequence registered positive in God's scales. Turmoil and tumult continued, the Philistines remained an existential threat, and the Divinely ordained priesthood became increasingly corrupt.

The story of Samuel is in large measure so familiar it needs little retelling. Specially trained to be a prophet and judge he was gifted intellectually with a sterling character and an historically admirable work ethic. By any measure he was a superlative judge of unflagging energy who brought honor and esteem to the office. Yet even he had his vulnerabilities for he was undermined by his two sons, Joel and Abijah. Samuel was confronted by a quandary faced by parents since time immemorial. How does a parent transmit his/her values and morals to the offspring? Samuel's sons were appointed judges themselves and were notorious for corruption, including the regular acceptance of bribes. Samuel's character and integrity and the administration of his office remained exemplary, but his sons had sullied the family name and also supplied an impetus to a political movement which was growing in Israel. This was the desire to improve God's plan and substitute a monarchial dynasty, i.e. a king, for the Divinely ordained judges. The Israelites desire was hardly rooted and drawing from great reservoirs of reason. Rather they simply wanted a king to be "like the other nations." Beset by centuries of problems from the degradation of Egyptian slavery and the purging in the Sinai wilderness to the rigors of bloody war in the conquest of Canaan and the hostility of surrounding nations the Israelites have now determined the source and root of all their problems – the form of government with which God has burdened them.

Some emotions make all mankind one and instill a kinship which any can understand, and undeniably one of those emotions at the top of the list is the fear of rejection. From newborn infancy to the burdens of age all want to be accepted. Childhood is a playground of thrills and happiness, but it is also a darkened cavern of fear and trepidation where lurk the evils and things we fear the most. Children fear, and too many rightly so, rejection by their parents. A child and even with greater intensity do adolescents and teenagers live in terror at the idea of not being accepted by their hoped-for friends and by various peer groups. Most intense of all is the deadening soul searing heartbreak of the young man or girl who is rejected by the one whose heart is sought. As the poet lamented, "Nothing is so sad as unrequited love."

All of these are real and bind human spirits together in ways many neither contemplate nor understand. Standing out from even the harshest of common rejections are a certain few emotional blows which are absorbed by only a few, and Samuel is reeling from this devastation. Here is a man, no longer young, whose entire existence from infancy has been consumed by his devotion and service to God and His people. Possessed of great innate ability and character he has given time, measured not in days or years but in decades, in service. One of the greatest prophets, incorruptible morally and impartial and indefatigable in his teaching of his countrymen he is to be unceremoniously tossed aside for the official stated reason that Samuel, "...Behold, thou art old." Samuel likely thought of all those years of service, the continual bone-wearying travel and the mental and emotional strains and imperatives of making judgments. Likely, as in all nations, eras and courts Samuel was working not just with serious issues of serious parties but rather litigants who seemingly were in heated competition to see who could be the most petty. He dealt with the high and mighty down to the mild and meek and performed well and tirelessly. His patience was likely taxed daily, and only the greatest of men could have performed so well and so long. Here is a man who from the cradle was dedicated to God's service by his mother Hannah and performed superlatively as the greatest of all Israel's judges. A different man he was, but Samuel merits comparison with Moses. What person so rejected would not be dejected and morose, and so it was with Samuel. It will be seen that Samuel would remain an integral component of God's plans and have vital duties, but for now let us turn to the one who, by any measure of reason, shall be bereft of patience.

We would not be remiss in identifying that generation of Israel which when hardened by the maelstrom of desert wanderings emerged loyal to God and loyal to God's chosen leader, Joshua, as perhaps Israel's own "greatest generation." Although they were mortal souls and not without faults and flaws, they maintained course and won victories. From that point of demarcation, though, Israel's history could be described as a line on a graph, at time gradually lowering and at times plunging precipitously into a quagmire of childishness, immorality and even idolatry. Yet God maintained His Divine demeanor of patience and continued to guide and guard the Chosen. His patience, elastic and flexible to an extreme, was stretched taut, and it held. It held when that of no man or woman would have done anything but break.

And now? Israel has a great, wise judge, selected by the Almighty Himself. At key moments God accorded brilliant and wise leadership in the persons of such as Deborah and Gideon. He had abided their whining ingratitude and the frequent apostasy into idolatry and still succored and sheltered them. Through these years, no, these centuries, we find that the definition of God and "long-suffering" are one and the same. So, Israel is in a tight spot, threatened by a nation highly skilled and experienced in warfare, and they, led by the elders of the nation, have concluded that their problem is a form of government. They have been saddled with a governmental structure of uniqueness, "...(not) like all the nations."

Although we are recollecting events of over three millennia past the similarities with all God's disciples in all nations, at all times and in all dispensations must here be highlighted. God chose the Hebrew people, saved them from slavery, rescued them repeatedly by signs and wonders and gave them nationhood and an abiding Law. The entire point, the Divine crux of the matter, is that they were not to be like other nations. As the Israelites are the Chosen so are Christians so referenced in our dispensation of time. In our age the Christian is guided by Paul's admonition:

"(B)e not conformed to this world: but be ye transformed by the renewing of your mind."

These are principles that few of the Israelites ever grasped. So now God is confronted with another moral dilemma, and He realizes wherein lay the real rejection and confronts Samuel:

"They have not rejected thee, but they have rejected me, that I should not reign over them."

A Creator now to be unceremoniously tossed down the memory hole, a Lord not wanted, a parent rejected by children. Humans have a finite limit to everything, including rejection, and ultimately any man or woman will find the bonds of a relationship broken, the patience drained and will turn away.

The popularly imagined wrathful and mythical "God of the Old Testament" would do all the above and far more. His wrath would be white hot in its intensity and this God would destroy His own with a flaming vengeance. Rejected and blamed this God's patience would have elapsed. It is now time to think of God as the Heavenly Father, with the emphasis on the second word. Every serious mother and father has suffered the emotional stress of parental exasperation, when the child has gone beyond the limits of patience and driven the parent to the brink of collapse. When parents reach this juncture several well worn options are available. The quickest refuge is a display of temper, even violent temper, but a considerable proportion of the time this is nothing less than a cathartic declaration of war upon the child. The total opposite is an abject surrender to the child, wherein the parent effectively washes his/her hands of the matter and with studied indifference turns the parental back to the child. Unsurprisingly, the ways of God not being the ways of men, He follows a different course. Through His prophet and judge Samuel He gently but clearly tells the people to "have it your way." Against all my desires, wishes, and Divine knowledge, you, my beloved children, are going to receive your King. God is expressing what parents have known for ages, that sometimes a father or mother is so worn down from battling the childish will that surrender seems to be the only course. By knowledge, experience and an almost instinctive sensibility a parent just "knows" that a child's chosen course of action will end in disaster. Yet the parent knows that nothing substantive can be done to thwart the child's misplaced ambition. He simply stands aside and laments "Have it your way," and witnesses the commencement of calamity. So, it was now with God, but not before the Lord expresses His views. Give them their King says God to Samuel but relate to them what monarchy will bring to them.

The Bible is many, many things, but it is not a textbook for governmental structure, civics or political science. Yet when it speaks here on this subject it is the fount of ultimate Divine wisdom. By all means, says God to Samuel, let them have their kings. In fact, I will aid them in the task of finding them, but do not be remiss in relating to them what pleasures will be theirs with their sparkling, glittering new monarchy. So, Samuel begins his dissertation in monarchy to the Israelites.

Your society will be less free he relates, as your sons will be conscripted into the King's armies for endless conflicts and wars. Your daughters will be taken for various tasks, labors and projects, all to the glory of the king. Kings will take what you always knew to be yours and the fruits of your labor, lands, livestock and crops. You will be the poorer for it, for he will allocate them to his own supporters, his lords, and your status as free will gradually evolve into a form of state vassalage. Taxes will increase sharply, and the results will not be your betterment but houses and monuments to the glory of the king. Finally, at the end of this reign of monarchial glory you will cry in despair to God, but He will not hear you. Simply and succinctly stated this is history first, and still its most eloquent warning against the dangers and hazards of "Big Government" unconstrained by traditions, virtue and law.

Yet God was still Israel's God, and His patience would be tried through the next few centuries. Moreover, so would Samuel's. In all societies and cultures and at all times when a person is dismissed from employment, told that their services are no longer needed, or more colloquially "fired" it is customary to exit the picture and the arena of activity. Not so with Samuel, though, because while the people thought they were better served without the old prophet's services God knew differently, and assigned him a major responsibility, one that would lay the bridge between the old way of the Judges and the new path of the Kings. Samuel was to notify and anoint the first of Israel's kings, a young man from the tribe of Benjamin, a man described as tall, handsome and impressive and named Saul. Thus, began the monarchial reign with some accomplishments, some glories and a few battlefield victories by both generally and specifically following the template of trial and tumult which God had set forth to Samuel. Eventually a divided nation would suffer the destruction and loss of ten of its twelve tribes, with the other two surviving in truncated form to suffer additional tribulations.

As will be seen God's patience at times will be pushed beyond its endurance, but generally Israel's history will offer a surfeit of Divine love and long-suffering. With Samuel the Lord had found one of His ideal servants, a man of copious abilities, loyalty and patience. As for God, yes, He was patient with the Israelites, but His patience ultimately will be revealed to have a greater purpose.

Chapter 3

NATHAN: CONFIDANTE AND CRITIC

*T*he initial returns were coming in rapidly, and it appeared that on this occasion the people of Israel were correct, and Samuel and his God were wrong. Not only had they apparently been proven wrong, but even more importantly they were not synchronized with those magical and majestic forces, known by various nomenclature but rather commonly as "the spirit of the times" or "the trend of history." Israel now truly was like all the other nations, but even more so, for it had its king, and what nation on earth had such a king. He was in the prime of his youth at age thirty and looked every bit the part. At a time and with a nation not known for the height of its inhabitants he was a dream come true. Described as a head taller than most other men Saul was strikingly handsome, no doubt muscular and the picture of virility gained from an outdoor life of vigorous farm and what today we would honor as "ranch work." In his early days he seemed to be blessed with a natural humility and modesty well becoming of any man in any station of life.

The nation state of Israel was unlike other nations of its (or really any) time, for its very right of existence was challenged by most of the other nations which abutted its very small perimeters. The same may be said for the modern twenty-first century state of Israel. For this as well as a veritable plethora of other reasons the young nation seemingly was always at war, often with more than one opponent simultaneously. Just as often those opponents were more numerous and had their roots into deeper and richer lodes of military tradition than did Israel. Israel wanted more than its distant and seemingly remote God and His aging and tired prophet Samuel. The people were desperate for a king that "...would go out before us, and fight our battles." They struck gold (nay, platinum, they must have thought), when Saul appeared and was crowned as their King. As much as any sovereign of antiquity Saul embodied the spirit of the warrior king, for especially in his reign's early years he expended more time and energy as a soldier than as a king. Wherever he turned his sword was gripped firmly in his strong hands, and Saul led the Israelites to many victories over the Ammonites, the Moabites and even the dread and omnipresent Philistines who were pressing from the west and the north.

Finally, King Saul led the Israelites to a great victory over a traditional foe, the Amalekites. Although it was a resounding military success it proved to be the beginning of the end. Commissioned by God to "utterly destroy" the Amalekites, man, woman, child and even the livestock the prideful spirit of Saul was demonstrated. His army was wildly successful and fulfilled in great part the Divine directive. The King, though, acting on his own initiative and in that always lurking human spirit of "I know better than God" he spared the life of the Amalekite king, Agag, and reprieved the lives of the Amalekite livestock, ostensibly to sacrifice to God. The victorious king returned from his field of glory with the conquered Agag and hordes of livestock in tow and who should he now confront but that figure who had presumably been consigned to the past, Samuel. Seeing Saul's spoils of war and the direct act of disobedience and rebellion it represented to the aged prophet and judge, shoved aside and shunned by the people, upon hearing Saul's fatuous explanation that he had come to offer sacrifice to God spoke these words, still oft-quoted today:

"Behold, to obey is better than sacrifice."

The glory of Saul's reign as king and as a man was short, for God had already taken the measure of the man. Endowed with great ability and not in any way lacking in personal virtues, God nevertheless turned from Saul because he had rejected God's desires in lieu of his own. God knew Saul's prideful, rebellious spirit, and God's patience with Saul was already at an end. Samuel informed Saul that "...the Lord hath rejected thee from being King over Israel." Although Saul would remain the ruler for many, many years to come, God's spirit had departed, and He sought not a dynastic monarchy in Saul's family but an entirely new King, this time "... a man after His own heart." Again, for this important task Samuel was selected and was dispatched to the home of a name named Jesse.

The choice of a humble shepherd youth named David, youngest son of Jesse, his spectacular emergence into the Biblical scene and his defeat of the Philistine giant, Goliath, has been told and related often and well that it needs no detailed recounting here. For the purposes of this writing, though, it is cogent and relative to remark about David's rise to fame and power and God's remarkable patience. David's first dramatic scene occurs in the valley of Elah, whereas an emboldened youth he slays Goliath. His age is scripturally unstated but likely in his early teens, and a long journey of fame, glory, glamour, misfortune, violence and treachery stretches before him before he attains the throne on the United Kingdom of Israel and Judah at the age of thirty-eight, a quarter century hence. David's patience was strained to its far reaches, but even more so was God's. In His Divine Wisdom He saw that years must elapse before David had added the needed maturity to his brilliance, and military circumstances had to evolve before both David and God were ready. Here is demonstrated what the mature person learns in that patience must often be exercised in unpleasant circumstances and in the blowing gales of adversity and tragedy, of which Israel and God suffered greatly in these years.

Well should God's suffering be great, and His reservoirs of patience drained by the jealousies of King Saul of the glamorous multitalented David. So bitterly did Saul's jealousies develop that three times he sought the death of David, was a hair's breadth short of killing his own son and David's dear friend Jonathan and converted his daughter into a pawn to be utilized in his death game against David. Moreover, Saul forced David into the fugitive life of an outlaw and turned his own kingdom into an arena for civil and internecine war. Yet, God's patience held.

Eventually the tragic life and downfall of Saul found his conclusion in his violent death on the battlefield. David soon became King of the southern tribes of Judah and Benjamin, and eight years later at the aforementioned age of thirty-eight King of all Israel. While the world may not have been David's the nation of Israel was so. What did the shepherd boy, now grown, do with it and was it pleasing to his Heavenly Father? He had a long reign, though one is loath to say that he "enjoyed" a long tenure as king. Succinctly stated he was the greatest of the kings of the United Kingdom, although the field was small as the only others were Saul and David's own son, Solomon. Yet his leadership abilities cannot be denied, his accomplishments were great and his legacy a lasting one. Truly in most respects he was a man and a king after God's own heart, even though as with us all his heart and intentions were at times misguided.

As God had foretold wars would be unceasing under the kings, and David's reign allowed little respite from this foretelling of the future. Little, but not none. During a break from the wars the King spoke to his companion, the prophet Nathan, and fretted that while he, David, as king luxuriated is a house of cedars, God's house of worship was a plain tabernacle that even lacked curtains. He hoped to build a house, a great house of worship for God, that would match any religious temple in the world. Nathan, doubtless charged and excited by David's enthusiasm, commiserated with the King and urged him "...do all that is in thine heart" and presumptuously, "...for the Lord is with thee." Speaking too hastily and out of turn is a part of the human condition, and all have made the error. Here, though, the error is made by an ordained prophet of God and directed to the King of God's Chosen nation, illustrating that even those we call "holy men" are liable to errors. For this God has patience, and the corrective course of action is given Nathan. He is instructed by God to advise the king that David was getting ahead of himself. Tell him that I took him from the sheepcote to rule over my people of Israel. At no time did I say to you, David, "Why build ye not me a house of cedar?" Nathan is to take David and guide him into a greater understanding than the "...Lord God dwelleth not in temples made with hands" and that He has far greater plans than the establishment of a building made with wood and stone. Nathan was to tell David that He would establish "...the throne of His Kingdom forever," a clear allusion to the establishment of His Church, and that a far greater King, Christ, would come from the lineage of David.

Of course, the great temple eventually was constructed in Jerusalem, but for a variety of circumstances and reasons not by David. Here, though, both David and Nathan have acted in a manner that has been and forever will be repeated innumerable times every day. Each has assumed without sufficient knowledge or evidence the will and intentions of another, and in this instance the offended party is God Himself. Even with the best intentions and with essentially good motives a person's (and God's) patience may be tried by forging ahead on a path of presumption. While God's patience and will has here been assumed God shows only correction and not wrath. He would allow the temple to be constructed, but in His own time and by His chosen vessel, in this case, David's son and kingly heir, Solomon.

This moment provides too good an opportunity to elapse without further expansion on the subject, and the subject is how God's patience must have been and is strained thought thousands of years by not only kings and agreeable prophets but also churches, priests and Christians who seek to memorialize Him by erecting earthly edifices. Unsurprisingly, God was correct in His anxieties and anticipations about the problems that would be generated by the construction of a temple. Obviously, its building was a great goal of David's but realized only during the reign of Solomon. It was later destroyed, though, and replaced and rebuilt in somewhat more subdued form later. It was the center of the Jewish faith, and in some manner had become an almost idolatrous center of Jewish worship by the time of Christ. In His teaching nothing could excite fevered opposition to Jesus from the Jewish hierarchy and religious establishment more than a perceived derogation of the temple by Christ. It had to a perception, though, because Christ taught openly in the temple and never attacked a mere building itself. He engendered such white-hot opposition that it helped lead to His crucifixion when He exclaimed that He would destroy the temple but then rebuild it within three days, an obvious metaphorical reference to His death, burial and resurrection but taken literally by many Jews. The Great Temple had become a fetish to many Jews, and one must wonder if they saw it less as a commemoration of God and more as a monument to themselves. Certainly, God knew of the dangers which would tempt His Chosen by having such a structure. Surely, we may ask has God's memory been altered in any manner and can He not foretell similar dangers in the Christian Age?

God is a God of many things and of many variations. He is a God of practicality, for in the life of His Son Jesus He demonstrated that He was aware of how people actually lived and got along day to day. By the creation of the world itself and its still unfolding magnificence He shows that He is a God of beauty. Further, the love of beauty in nature and in structure is seemingly inherent in humanity. The majority wishes to dwell in "nice" houses and have "nice" items of property and live "nice" lives. A nice place of worship fits well within this template, and mankind has almost outdone itself in this regard. For century upon century some of the most beautiful of structures have been imagined, constructed and dedicated to Divine Worship. A reasonable, thinking person would with difficulty be required to fashion an argument that there exists any intrinsic wrong in a magnificent cathedral or a beautiful modern structure. But the question begs to be asked – are these constructed for the glory of the Creators or for the glories of the building creators? Back to 1000 B.C., though, and the same question must be asked relative to two legitimately great and genuinely sincere servants of God, Nathan and Davie. Would God be glorified by this, or would it more accurately be seen as burnishing the glittering reputation of David. Both men overstepped the parameters of their roles, but God, again whose patience was great, readjusted David's designs. King David's reign and Nathan's prophecies continued.

Whatever mistakes David made with his desire to build a temple undoubtedly his heart was in the right place. Unfortunately, David's heart possessed a particular mobility, which led to one of the most infamous stories in all of history and temporarily his abandonment of God. Even today, the believing Christian contemplates the story, the deviousness, cruelty and criminal acts of David and wonders if God's patience with any one person in the Old Testament was ever tested greater or with more intensity. It is, of course, the tale of the tryst with Bathsheba, the succession of sins and crimes and the degeneracy of David's moral character. No less is it the story of Nathan's courage and of God's mercy. This is a narrative which has been told and retold, dramatized and analyzed so often and often so well that its repetition, except in summary form, is not needed here.

At the pinnacle of his fame and power King David stays in his palace home while his generals and soldiers go forth to fight his battles for him. One evening his mid-life desires aroused by the sight of a beautiful young woman bathing, he impels her to come to him. His passion is requited and to his chagrin Bathsheba, a married woman, becomes pregnant. A series of events occurs wherein David swiftly descends a ladder of immorality. Already having been an adulterer he compounds his sin repeatedly by ordering one of his finest officers, Uriah, murdered in the heat of battle. An act of treason itself, in David's thoughts it was justified by Uriah's being the husband of Bathsheba. Thankfully, it was all over, David still had his reputation and kingdom intact and as a wonderful bonus the beautiful Bathsheba, who now became his bride and bore him a new son. Throughout it all a Divine silence reigned, until the chronicler Samuel spoke these words:

"But the thing that David had done displeased the Lord."

This is perhaps the greatest understatement in the history of articulated language.

Nathan, a man of whom we know little if none apart from his prophetic life and returns to the scene as God's agent and a dark harbinger for David. Nathan relates a quite interesting and appropriate story for David, the former shepherd boy. A vile rich man had impinged upon the goodness of a humble man, a poor soul who had but one sheep that he raised as a pet, so close to him that the sheep was a daughter receiving his love. The wealthy man threw a banquet for his friends, slaughtered the poor man's pet and served it to his guests. So livid with righteous anger was David that he proclaimed that the rich man who sunk to such depravity should die. Nathan's simple, courageous and overpowering calamitous reply:

"Thou are the man."

We should be reluctant to ever state that God has "lost His temper," which implies a loss of control which is not God's nature. No one would be remiss, though, that God "has lost His patience." How sorely had David tempted God, far beyond the breaking point for any of us and, for that matter, any mortal man. Yet God's patience, even with the chosen is not limitless and of eternal endurance. Perhaps the purest example of God's patience shaping with an individual who has tried Him to the breaking point is found here. Yet while David had no pity upon Uriah, God still displays pity and mercy to David. What follows is the Old Testament illustration which more than any one event demonstrates the difference between the patience of man and the patience of God. When perusing and then delving more deeply into this story the disciple of God invariably loses his patience. David, a man who has achieved fame, wealth, power and women all while under the protection of God haughtily and disgustingly tosses it all aside because of his desire for the wife of another man. Effectively David has recklessly romped through the Ten Commandments under which he lives and broken every one in his pursuit of Bathsheba. Adultery, lying, covetousness, theft and murder have all been visited and deeply explored by David. From the finger of God Himself the Law of Moses recognizes the punishment of death for the enormity of his crimes and sins. Any serious steadfast Israelite or believing Christian has both an intellectual and almost visceral desire to see David pay with his life.

The patience and wisdom of God is different, though, and as always, He sees the panorama of the bigger picture. Neither Israel nor humanity as a whole has yet been redeemed, and the lineage of David has an integral part to play. God decrees that David shall live but that "...the sword shall never depart from thine house." David, the man and the King, has much life remaining but it will be lived in pain and sorrow. Later, a man known by many names, not least of which was Son of David, would explain to His followers "...all they that take the sword shall perish with the sword." In David's life God was to demonstrate the uniqueness of this principle applied to David, for he would perish a multiplicity of times. He perished soon thereafter when the baby carried by Bathsheba died. The King died again when his son Amnon committed incest with his sister Tamar. He perished when his son Absalom then murdered Amnon for Amnon's incestuous rape of his sister. And yes, he suffered when Absalom led a rebellion which almost took the throne from David but was then killed by David's general, Joab. Maybe or likely especially the vengeance which God exacts can be harsher than any man can inflict.

As for Nathan he remains even today a man and a prophet primarily known for one confrontation and that with a man he served, and no doubt honored. Even more so, though, his fame likely is based upon the simple but sledgehammer effect of four words, "Thou art the man." From God's retention of Nathan, even after David's death, we may be confident that he always retained favor.

With David's death an era ended, and more troubles and hard times lay ahead for Israel. Very hard times, which would showcase for all time both God's patience and the limitation of His patience. Yet, as the great story continues apace, we learn that His patience is not reserved for Israel alone.

Chapter 4

THE LONG AND WINDING ROAD

The succession of a nation's head of state has so often been a confused, tumultuous affair and a point in time in which personal, ethnic and national feelings burn with a consumptive intensity. Increasingly in the modern era the replacement of presidents and prime ministers uncovers the worst in a society (or at least in its aspirants for high office), but thankfully in recent generations this has rarely been accompanied (at least in nations enjoying advanced political systems) by personal and national bloodletting. Even a cursory knowledge of history, though, reveals that often kings, presidents and national leaders assume office only after treading or in some cases wading through streams and rivers of blood. For a long time, however, this was not something which characterized God's Chosen People, the Israelites. This was so during the period in which God selected and ruled through the judges, and although the record of these leaders is at times uneven and even disappointing seldom was it marked by brother shedding brother's blood. Yes, but Israel demanded its king, and God granted His children their wish. With the kings came bloodshed, and especially was it so marked when one king died, and others sought the crown. All this was foretold by the prophet Samuel when Israel made the transition into monarchy, so must God's patience have been strained when it happened recurrently and especially upon the death of King David.

Almost everyone from the great and the good to the humble and lowly expected David's successor as king to be his son Adonijah, the remaining eldest of David's almost twenty sons. Even prior to David's death Adonijah was ceremonially proclaimed the royal heir. A few others thought differently, though. Soon, aided by his mother and David's widow, Bathsheba, and the old prophet Nathan, the younger son of David, Solomon, was proclaimed king. The tide of public opinion shifted, and Adonijah saw that he no longer possessed sufficient support to hold the crown. As a kind of peace offering and a consolation prize, he requested from his half-brother Solomon a beautiful young girl Abishai, a member of the royal harem. Since the harem's bounty belonged to the king only young Solomon saw this request as an attempted usurpation of his royal rights. Thus, he had Adonijah executed (or more properly, "murdered") and now possessed a throne safe, at lease temporarily, from the grasping clutching hands of others.

Many political reigns begin their lives in the sunlit uplands, and such is not just reserved for those figures who history reveres. Two of the most despicable and historically despised emperors which ancient Rome endured were Caligula and Nero, each of whose reign fell in the first century. Today each name is synonymous with corruption, cruelty and debauchery, yet it is not difficult to find words of praise in the early stages of rule, when each appeared to take their office soberly and had genuine concern for the well-being of their subjects. The murderer of many wives, the infamous King Henry VIII of England, was a cultured, intellectually astute figure who had the best interests of his Kingdom at heart in his early years before he finally became morally degenerate.

Young King Solomon started well, perhaps brilliantly, and presided over a kingdom during the Golden Age, when in many outward respects, Israel achieved its greatest pinnacles of glory. Seemingly, he was an odd choice for such an exalted position as King of Israel. Only twenty-four years old, he had no particular training or exposure to governing, and in a time and place of war he was fully lacking in military experience. A casual observer could well conclude that he attained his position by being the son of his father's favorite wife, Bathsheba. Solomon, though, was in no sense bereft of natural gifts and advantages. His reign consumed four decades of the historical life of Israel, and only the most severe and willfully unknowing critic could deny that the man had a great and keen intelligence. Of itself, though, while great intelligence may be highly advantageous, to employ the common vernacular smart people "...are a dime a dozen." Much more importantly, though, is another moral and mental quality for which the name Solomon is synonymous even today. In the early morning of his rule God asked of Solomon what he most desired, and Solomon responded "wisdom". So it was that Solomon's desire was fulfilled, and through the centuries the phrase "as wise as Solomon" has become an idiomatic element of our language. The stories of Solomon's wisdom became widely known, even legendary. Visiting ambassadors and even monarchs commented on the wisdom whereby he governed his land.

In an earthly, almost literal sense, Solomon built Israel. Certainly, his most memorable and magnificent achievement was the construction and dedication of the edifice which had been denied his father David, the great and magisterial temple in Jerusalem. On a day thoroughly recorded in the book of I Kings the Temple was dedicated to the glory of God, and Solomon himself gave a moving, superlative speech. Many have noted this day as the highpoint of Israel as a nation in the ancient days. As much as political affairs can ever be the state of the nation was excellent. Still, Solomon was not through in his constructive designs. The face of Israel was changing, with new structures made from fine woods and metals appearing. Israel was strong, even for a small nation, and for a long tenure it faced no excessively formidable military enemy, as it had done for centuries. Further, of great value both domestically and externally, this tiny nation was more unified than at any time since the great days of Joshua. Like almost all nations at any time Israel was a blend of more than one people, of multiple cultures, ideas, traditions and ways of daily living. All Israelites maintained a great commonality, but still it was a land of twelve tribal peoples, and often they got along no better than the twelve sons of Jacob for whom they were named. Yet their differences under the young King Solomon appear to have receded somewhat, and it was truly a united nation, a United Kingdom under Solomon.

At this juncture the observer is almost compelled to utter the question that we dare not thing, much less speak. Had God been wrong about the King? Israel appeared far stronger, more unified and greater than at any time during the long succession of judges. Were the words which God shared with Samuel to be consigned to the bleak memories of dark days when Israel was wedded to an ancient religion, an old-fashioned system of government and a God best forgotten? The answer to all these questions is a divinely resounding "No" pealing throughout both Heaven and Earth. Yes, an old cliché really was true in that appearances are deceiving. Although Israel was shiny and even glittering, taking its rightful place in the panoply of the world's powers, the rot and moral degeneracy had begun and would not stop until most of the nation had been destroyed and only a relative handful of Jews remained, a "remnant".

Solomon was a man of great ability and accomplishment, yet he presided over the last of the United Kingdom of Israel, a kingdom before which lay a long and winding road to destruction. All those warnings of the dangers of monarchy seemed to a people, ravenous in their desire for a king, as the demented ramblings of the tired old prophet Samuel. Yet they were now coming true, and not just in a generalized sense, but with a precision and exactitude which made Samuel – well, a prophet. Samuel's first prophecy was likely the first fulfilled. Israel was warned that its King would conscript their sons for his vastly expanded army and as drivers of his new chariots. Solomon did create a mobile corps of charioteers, which required thousands of drivers. As for the army, then as now a great king and a great government required a great army. Military conscription, the "draft" became an ancient tyranny for the glory of Kings. Hordes of young men were torn from their chosen occupations and paths in life not necessarily for the defense of their country, but for the glory of the King.

True, the Temple and other structures enhanced the image of Israel and its reputation, but these came at a serious price. They were not executed with voluntary contracted labor, but rather with forced servitude, a more elegant way of saying slavery. The mass of the Israelites was again subjected to bondage to build edifices to the glory of God. Pharaoh? Or perhaps King Solomon. The bitter irony that the passage of centuries had led from Egypt to Israel and from slavery to ...slavery. Taxes on produce, livestock, grain and all manner of production had increased under King David and now skyrocketed under King Solomon. Yet, as bad, tragic and predictable as was this compendium of predicted woes, Israel survived, and even prospered.

The Kingdom of Israel indeed was united under King Solomon, but it was a unity which any tyrant or despot would recognize, envy and admire. The government bureaucracy burgeoned under Solomon and the inevitable swarm of administrators, officials and bureaucrats descended upon the land, all with the intent, explicit or implicit, direct or indirect, of enhancing the status and rule of the monarchy. Even the small country of Israel, while ostensibly united, was subdivided into administrative districts for easier control and governance from Jerusalem. To showcase his power and further antagonize his subjects Solomon directed that the boundary lines for these districts be drawn without regard to the ancient borders of Israel's twelve tribes, a needless act of contempt to tradition, the people and most importantly to God. In almost every phase and facet Israel had truly become Solomon's possession and his kingdom, and he and his dynastic succession seemingly were set for an almost interminable reign. How wrong he was.

No matter how glorious the Temple, no matter the pomp and circumstance of the King and his cortege and regardless of his reputation and strength of his army, Solomon's kingdom and dynasty were beginning to rot. It is to be surmised that the decay was proximately caused by two factors, one directly related and leading to the other. Be he prince or pauper, king or knave, any man must control his personal appetites, and this very much includes and in most instances is in the fore, his sexual desires and passions for women. Solomon had no control, and this is an absolute in that his life showed no check on his desire for women. This did not lead to one or two adulteries or dalliances, but rather the full sordid splendor of the lifestyle of an eastern potentate. The great, noble Solomon was of course, the son of King David, who himself offered an abysmal example in his dealings with women, adulteries and multiple affairs. Like father, like son, but Solomon partook of his affairs in a different dimension. The Book of I Kings records that he maintained a royal harem of 700 wives and 300 concubines. However, one may wish to quibble over the exactness of these numbers the point is well made Biblically. The person of Solomon contained a voracious, even insatiable, appetite for women, and he doubtlessly used them as much as any man who ever lived. This is emanating from God's chosen ruler, a man who is the son of a king described as a man after God's own heart. Whether by degrees or by immoral deluges, Solomon's character and personal morality had collapsed. Sadly, even grotesquely this was not the worst of it. Whatever moral depredations suffered by Solomon, or to whom his influence was a strong factor, they are pushed into the background, into the shade by what accompanied them, as the Old Testament relates:

> "...(H)is wives turned away his heart after other gods: and his heart was not perfect with the Lord his God, as was the heart of David his father."

Solomon was a man of varied taste, craving the beautiful feminine riches of all nations to be his wives. With these wives came their religions, which Solomon not only tolerated, but accommodated. The various gods and goddesses of other lands, the deities of the Egyptians, the Canaanites, the Philistines and others now had their altars and temples in Israel, where great numbers of the Jews began to worship. The long road which led from Egypt, the land of Pharaoh, slavery and pagan idolatry had wound its way to the Promised Land of Israel, which effectively had its own overreaching Pharaoh and enough heathen idols to satisfy any soul. Still, God's patience held, and His wrath was stayed.

We humans presently are earth bound and tied to this world both physically and emotionally, and none of us can know the unrevealed mind of God. Still we are almost driven at times to speculative thought. How did God really feel now? Solomon had been the favored son of David and David's favorite wife Bathsheba, likely the only one for whom he had real feelings of love. His life was protected from infancy through young adulthood, given a United Kingdom in the sunshine of its existence and great wisdom with which to govern it. Seemingly, if not overlooking his behaviors, God tolerated Solomon's tyranny, his self-glorification and his often-egocentric behavior. He neither could nor would have patience with Solomon's truly fulfilling a previous generation's plea that "we be like other nations," and so they were. Solomon, slowly at first, and then quickly opened the floodgates to idolatry and paganism and all that went with it. For at least six centuries more it was a plague, a self-imposed bacillus, on the Jewish people. Eventually they rid themselves of this destroyer but not before the bulk of the populace had suffered slavery, even genocide, and destruction with only a small remnant remaining. Solomon was not alone responsible, but the road of destruction went through his royal palace.

Similar to most rulers of any era, whether royal or common, Solomon sought to extend his reign and glory by the creation of a dynastic succession. His sons were, in fact, his successors, but neither had any of Solomon's partially admirable qualities. Yet they provided some modicum of relief for Solomon. God was ready to take the Kingdom from King Solomon, but due to Solomon's being the son of David this humiliation was withheld from Solomon. It would not be so with the two men, one a son, who followed him.

To the modern ear the names intone a rig of artificiality, and upon first hearing them they possess a semi-serious, even comical sound. Yet in reality nothing was comic or laughable when it came to the two successors of Solomon, Jeroboam and Rehoboam, the latter being "legitimate" successor to Solomon and the United Kingdom of Israel, who took the reigns perhaps as a co-ruler even before his father's passing. To Rehoboam fell the burden and fury of confronting and ruling an Israelite people who had grown weary of the imposition of Solomonic burdens of military conscription, forced labor and excessive taxation. They were poised to erupt in insurrection, and the older, wiser counselors of Rehoboam knew this. Yet it was not inevitable, for the patience of God is of almost infinitely elastic strength, and God has often changed His mind. Wisely, Rehoboam's advisers told the King:

"If thou wilt be a servant unto this people this day,
and will serve them, and speak good words to them,
then they will be thy servants indeed."

Wise words indeed, and if kings, presidents, prime ministers, rulers and leaders of all sorts would heed them what a different world this would be. Unfortunately for Israel Rehoboam was most definitely one of those rulers. He was, however, not entirely bereft of at least a modicum of intelligence. Many of the tribal leaders were keenly attune to the people and knew that they were on the verge of rebellion after the long oppression of Solomon's rule. Instead of Jerusalem as the place of Rehoboam's coronation they insisted upon the old northern city of Shechem. Jerusalem was the capital, was the locus of the Temple and the focal point for most of Solomon's construction, with the great buildings rising from the blood, sweat and toil of these people. His crowning there would be a bitter reminder of their years of oppressive slavery.

The Israelites, however, were soon relieved of any notions that the Kingdom of son Rehoboam would be any less strenuous than that of father Solomon. Rehoboam listened not to his older counselors, the leaders of the twelve tribes, who cautioned that a moderate spirit would be best in a king. Instead, he eagerly lapped up the advice of his younger companions who urged a hardline policy against his own people, an ancient reign of terror. With relish Rehoboam spoke:

"My father made your yoke heavy, and I will add to
your yoke: my father also chastised you with whips,
but I will chastise you with the scorpions."

The threatened "scorpions" were bits of bone, stone and metal placed in the lashes of the whip to make the sufferer's punishment more unbearable. Israel now lay at the feet of not just a tyrant but a sadist. All this became too onerous for the Israelite leadership to tolerate, and they left Rehoboam. Plans were now being made and instituted for the secession of the northern tribes from the Kingdom. As much as any point, this may be taken as the moment when the United Kingdom of Israel ceased to exist and as a nation-state ceased to exist forever. Allowed by a highly reluctant God, He had now, after the reigns of only three kings, Saul, David and Solomon, witnessed a nation that He had fashioned from hordes of Egyptian slaves pull itself apart – point by point, principle by principle, horror by horror, Israel had richly fulfilled all of God's warnings spoken through the prophet Samuel. Yet He remained their God. Truly in the purest and most literal meaning of the word His patience was Divine.

So now what would become of the seceded ten northern tribes? Their secession, to any contemporary observer, would not have been shocking for politically, emotionally and even religiously a rift between the ten and the two southern tribes had begun to form and grow toward the end of Solomon's reign. With apparent fortune the ten tribes (henceforth still called "Israel" so opposed to the southern "Judah") had a young, exciting leader in this secession, a man named Jeroboam. Solomon himself had been aware of the danger of this potential usurper and in the living testimony to the adage that history repeats itself, he attempted unsuccessfully to kill Jeroboam, as King Saul had tried with Solomon's father David.

After a time of strife Jeroboam was successful in having the ten northern tribes coalesce around his person and leadership and he became the king of a new Israel. Many leaders are popular at the outset simply because they are new, or because people want them to be popular, giving them a chance to succeed. So, it was with Jeroboam, but the "honeymoon" was of short duration. Literally did Jeroboam's name become a by ward for sin and evil, and it echoed through generations of history. No less than twenty times does the Bible employ the phrase "...walked in the way of Jeroboam" to describe a kind of apotheosis of evil. So why was Jeroboam so bad? Our theme does not require the details, but succinctly expressed Jeroboam sought to construct a new political and religious order in Israel, an order made in Jeroboam's image. He created a new priestly caste, deliberately disregarding the Levites, the divinely ordained priesthood, and most legitimate Levite priests fled to Jerusalem in Judah. Jeroboam was personally more oppressive than Solomon and the equal to his rival despot Rehoboam. His dynasty was short, and perished in less than a quarter century, yet he established a precedent in the new northern Kingdoms of Israel. Israel would never, never have a good king.

Where God had promised one united people under judges chosen by Him alone now stood a divided Kingdom of two discontented groups, the ten northern tribes of Israel and the largest of the twelve, Judah, in the south. The twelfth tribe of Benjamin, adjacent to both Israel and Judah would provide a battlefield for a civil war between the two kingdoms, with Judah eventually winning and Benjamin joining its southern neighbor. The peoples of Israel and Judah were bound by a common history, a common blood and a common promise, but their paths now began to diverge. The blessing and promise made to Abraham long ago in Genesis still held, though, and that promise renewed through Moses, the judges and King David still held true and fast. The Chosen Seed had poorly handled, even bungling to near destruction, the great promise. The patience of God had been tried many times beyond human comprehension, yet He remained firm in His commitments. The winding road of fulfillment, begun so long ago, remained lengthy still. It contained endless twists, turns, points of peril and even destruction, but the road remained. The road continued, apparently but not actually, divided into two forks now. Not even God's prophets knew that it would find a destination known but to God.

› Chapter 5 ‹

THE SOUNDS OF SILENCE

inally, the northern tribes of Israel had thrown off the shackles of being bound to its southern neighbor, Judah. Gone was the dynasty and the lineal succession of kings from David, Solomon and Rehoboam, for those belonged solely to the south. Although they had scorned these centuries of promise and tradition, they were still no ordinary nation. Underlying the desires and actions of Israel's kings and its populace was a desire to break with God completely and be "...like the other nations." For two centuries Israel walked a perilous course and wavered between the diversity of a multiplicity of gods and religions, even including the worship of Jehovah, to outright apostasy and rejection of God. Once again, though God had been ignored, the subject of ridicule and humiliation, His patience remained, and Israel clung to its independence for another two centuries. God yet dispatched holy prophets with a message of truth, but they remained subjects of derision and persecution. The northern kingdom had its days in the sun and material prosperity was by no means a stranger to the nation. Still, God's patience remained with Israel for a full two centuries before the land and people met their ultimate destruction. These events and God's reaction through His prophets' merit closer scrutiny, and to this we will return. For now, though, what of the southern tribes of Judah and Benjamin, those that did not secede and ostensibly, at least, remained true to God and His promise?

The names Abijah, Asa, Jehosophat, Jehoram, Ahaziah, Athaliah, Jehoash and Amaziah do not glide and slide smoothly off the modern English-speaking tongue. This proposition should excite little wonder, for this is a list of the first kings which followed Rehoboam on the still (but barely) intact throne of David in Judah. They are an interesting group of men, but hardly are they in the front rank of famous Old Testament characters. Under these men the monarchy at times plummeted to immoral depths, but Judah still claimed periods of allegiance to God under some of the better of the Kings. Unlike Israel, Judah did enjoy the experience of, at times, living under good kings. Another dissimilarity to their northern brothers is that although Judah was plagued by idols and heathen worship and immorality, it never completely abandoned God, as did Israel. The true story of all this is the Old Testament itself, and this small work is meant only to draw light to certain persons and events. A scholarly review of the period requires a scholastic, deep and lengthy study, many of which exist.

Yet another group of names Biblically followed the previously mentioned Kings of Judah. These are the names of Uzziah, Jotham, Ahaz and Hezekiah, the four men who next assumed the throne in order of succession. They are grouped together in the first verse of one of the Bible's longest and most important books, Isaiah. This man Isaiah was not the first of Judah's prophets nor was he the first to achieve historical and Biblical fame, for he was preceded by many others, notably Zechariah and Joel, each of whom authored Old Testament books and gained notoriety as prophets. Isaiah's time was in the eighth century B.C., and unlike the prophets in the northern kingdom Isaiah was able to enjoy working with at least one good king, the renown Hezekiah, a man of great ability and one who possessed a drive to please God. Unfortunately, however, the bulk of Isaiah's work was with bad kings and a multitude of Judah which overwhelmingly neglected God or even attempted to purge Him and His followers root and branch from the country's culture.

Isaiah remains a man known more for his prophecy than for his life, which must be assembled piecemeal from Biblical and historical scraps, archaeological finds and traditional stories. The narrative of his life is mortgaged to assumptions and the few facts we glean from scriptures. He is an enigmatic character, but a man of whom we read is all good and praiseworthy. This places him on a short roster of Old Testament men and women, perhaps a shorter list than many persons imagine. From the outset we are confronted with both fact and supposition concerning this vague figure of a man. From the lengthy sixty-six-chapter Book of Isaiah many certainties are revealed though. Isaiah was an artfully skilled craftsman of the Hebrew language, and scholastic opinion has long ago developed a consensus that his writing is the most elegant and graceful found in the entire Bible. It certainly suggests a man of great intellectual gifts, likely polished by a fine, perhaps even royal, education. As for this, it has been suggested in Jewish tradition that Isaiah was the brother of King Amaziah, making him a cousin of the more famed King Uzziah. In any event, though inspired, the instrument of God's inspiration was a man of great ability, who could craft sentences and phrases widely quoted almost three millennia hence. Isaiah's voice rings loudly even today, and it is no mere enthusiasm to state that he is the most frequently cited and influential prophet of the Bible.

The great omnipresent reality of Isaiah's life and prophecy is the reality of how ineffective he was in his own lifetime in the 700's B.C. His speech and writings were directed towards both his contemporaries and future generations extending to the present. He remains studied, quoted, admired and even revered by Christians yet today.

From his fellow citizens, though, he met opposition, scorn, hatred and but a tiny element of need and admiration. Isaiah's story (and it is played out over a long and full life) is a tale of God's patience once again being tried, but also the patience and frustration Isaiah was required to endure. None of the Old Testament's major figures seemingly and apparently has less to show for a lifetime's hard, perilous labor than did Isaiah. We quote, though, one of history's oldest (but) true cliché s when we offer the retort that "Appearances are deceiving." Has a person who expends most of the precious gift of life walking against the grain, confuting the tide of "politically" and morally correct opinion wasted his life by maintaining a positive attitude towards the future against all available evidence a fool? By being patient with both man and with your God for a lifetime of opprobrium and being discarded the mission of a fool? Finally, did God waste the life of a great prophet by calling out such a prophet and burdening Isaiah as He did? The Bible is an endless compilation of stories where the patience of men and women and certainly that of God is rewarded. Yet, any sentient being knows that patience is not always rewarded, at least in this life. Both Isaiah's life and his prophecy call for closer scrutiny.

As was shown Isaiah's mission was to Judah in the south, but these southern Jews were not heedless or impervious to the events in the north. When Isaiah came on the scene Israel was a kingdom which was entering its final phase of dissolution. Its aggressive and expansive northern neighbor had its sights on the conquest of Israel. Assyria, among all the ancient warlike peoples, was virtually in a class of its own when it came to aggression, brutality and savagery. They were feared by all, and the gaping Assyrian ambition promised to soon swallow Israel whole. Thus, did the fate of their northern brothers and sisters offer a sinister warning of what possibly lay in store for a Judah that was remiss in its loyalty to God. Isaiah's entrance upon the stage comes during a vision, a divine manifestation, wherein he sees God and trembles at the feared doom which awaits one who has lain eyes on the Divine. Instead God absolves Isaiah of any guilt and poses to him the question of who shall God send as a prophet. He secures from Isaiah, undoubtedly a very young man at this time the following simple pledge:

"Here am I; send me."

God had found His man and along with Elijah and Jeremiah perhaps the most famous of the Old Testament prophets. His commission to Isaiah was by no means unique, and it aligned easily with those given to the other prophets. At the risk of sounding overly simplistic it was basically the still extant message of live well morally, worship God alone and shun idolatry. It was not the message that had quality of singularity, though, but rather God's portent of what the people's reaction would be. God's commission included the following words of warning to Isaiah:

> "Go, and tell this people, Hear ye indeed, but understand not; and see ye indeed, but perceive not."

From the Divine to the plainest of human speech Isaiah is being told to prophesy but expect no positive response. This is akin to an employer telling his sales personnel to go on the road, demonstrate the product but never expect any sales. Or perhaps a surgeon telling a roomful of patients that he will give them his best efforts, but they are all going to die anyway. It is simply a stunningly remarkable message to relay to a prophet as he receives his commission. Since our theme is patience may we not inquire of the nature and depth of character required to accept such a commission? Whatever wellsprings of virtue and patience Isaiah was to draw upon they were deep indeed.

Individual men and women are found to ignore advice, even and maybe especially good advice, every moment of everyday, and such will always be. It is simply part and parcel of the human condition, as much in our time as it was in the ancient days of Isaiah. Disregarding or even opposing good advice may often lead down a path to bad, even horrible, consequences. Generally, though, most of humanity has always led private lives, and while our lives intersect and entwine with others the consequences of our actions usually (but not always) have an effect upon ourselves and a few others only. While Isaiah was a prophet to multitudes he is also to be remembered as a prophet to the kings and the other assorted "high and mighty". Kings, presidents, prime ministers and other heads of state and the holders of the reigns of power are different. Should they ignore good advice the consequences may be both immediate and long-lasting, widespread, dire and disastrous. Isaiah likely issued prophecies and expositions of God's designs and desires to more Kings than did any other prophet. He was ignored, scorned, ridiculed, humiliated and persecuted, and perhaps it is likely that he was even martyred. No greater exemplar or royal intransigence disregard for good advice and the stupidity of following blindly one's own prejudicial thinking is to be found than in the story of one of the less familiar of Judah's kings, a monarch named Ahaz.

Assuming the throne at the tender age of twenty Ahaz's character, ability and intelligence advertised their proprietor as essentiality a boy fulfilling the office of a man. In short, he was out of his depth, and he and his nation were confronted by foreign crises of gargantuan proportions. The Assyrian Empire was hoping to continue its relentless expansive advance, and to counter its power Ahaz was asked to ally Judah with the nations of Syria and Israel, to stem the Assyrian tide. He refused, and was then attacked by both, with the capital of Jerusalem itself being besieged. Now, evidencing that politics and alliances in the ancient world could be just as changing and alliances just as evanescent as in the modern, Ahaz now pondered an alliance with the dread Assyria so as to repel Israel and Syria.

Enter Isaiah the prophet, whose diplomatic portfolio was not as representative of any nation or alliance but as the voice of the ancient God of Israel. Isaiah strongly urged that Ahaz abandon any concept of Judah's alliance with apostate Israel or Gentile kings, but rather lead His people in a return to the reliance upon and worship of the one true God. Ahaz, scared, basically incompetent and too reluctant to trust the prophet then turned to an act, an abomination so repulsive that regretfully the old adage of "truth is stranger than fiction" was proved again. King Ahaz ordered the sacrifice of his own son's life and "... even burned his son as an offering" in a bizarre display of twisted logic that would somehow compel God's wrath not upon his royal self but rather upon Judah's enemies. Seemingly, the desire of Ahaz could not be sated by a mere dramatic murder of his own son, but he also prostrated himself and his nation before the king of Assyria, begging that Judah be saved from its enemies. Ahaz himself traveled to the city of Damascus to pay tribute to the Assyrian king and to worship at the altars of the Assyrian gods. So impressed was he by the great Damascus pagan altar was Ahaz that he gave orders that such an altar be replicated in Jerusalem where sacrifices to the "gods of Damascus" would be offered. Not only had King Ahaz pushed the accelerator to the moral and spiritual crumbling of Judah, but also by the time he had imperiled his country by acquiescing in it becoming a vassal state to the great Assyrian Empire. All because he would not listen to God speaking through the voice of Isaiah. How God's patience must have been strained and pulled taut by the apostate Ahaz. Yet it held still, although Judah was in imminent danger, a quasi-slave state subservient to Assyria.

As if to shock Judah and its apostate subjects God ordained Isaac, a man of education and elegance, to now dress and walk among the people in a manner to catch the attention of anyone. He began to dress in a fashion that has come to be associated (often incorrectly) with the prophets. Isaac set aside his outer garment and adorned only in rough sackcloth and barefoot in the bargain began to circulate and teach amidst the populace, the upper class of which, including the priesthood, had begun to become accustomed to fine, soft living and elegant, fashionable dress. Ahaz and his cohorts had not acted out of fear of God in their apostasy, but rather fear of their enemies and had begun to worship idols to placate their powerful heathen masters. Isaiah saw that more and more the Jews had not followed the Assyrian gods out of fear but rather their growing belief in paganism.

For all this, though, at the death of Ahaz, Judah was on the verge of collapse. Israel in 722 B.C. had fallen victim to the seemingly unstoppable enemy from the north, and a weakening Judah seemed too weak to avoid a similar fate. Yet, King Ahaz had another son who had not been offered to the Assyrian deities. Remarkably, with a father of the caliber of Ahaz, his son assumed the throne at age twenty-five and became one of the two great kings in Judah's history. His name was Hezekiah, and as much as his father was given to Judah's destruction and extinction so Hezekiah was to its reform and redemption. In the plain language of the Old Testament Hezekiah:

"...held fast to the Lord; he did not depart from Him."

Hezekiah instituted a desperately required redemption of the Temple, removing Canaanite images from the landscape, reinstituting the religious practices and traditions of the Law of Moses and once more honoring God in word, thought and deed. With all that Hezekiah remained a mortal king with a man's limitations, for he did not touch the great altar which Ahaz had constructed in the Temple, no doubt believing he could go only so far with his people. Religious revival and redemption was wonderful, but the political skies were darkening for Judah. Assyria had come into the hands of the historically famous King Sennacherib, a man of brilliance and enormous talents. Assyrian armies were on the march and began to make vassals of states along the Mediterranean seacoast. Finally, the host of Assyria lay siege to Jerusalem and Sennacherib eyed another jewel to add to his crown, and to best the tribute of the literal jewels and precious metals held in the Temple. The best laid plans of mice, men and kings oft go astray, and in a spectacular victory the army of Judah smashed and obliterated the Assyrian threat. So, at last seemingly the Lord's apparently unending patience with Judah was to be rewarded, with a good devout king in office, a revitalized and repentant nation and a loyal prophet to serve Him. Sadly, Hezekiah seems to be a historical and spiritual, aberration, for he was soon succeeded by his son, Manasseh, and the old, old story of apostasy and paganism was to be retold with Manasseh as the new protagonist Manasseh, though, seemed to have a strong feel for the "good old days" for he was not satisfied with the gods and goddesses of the Assyrians. He reintroduced the deities, the "abominable practices" of the land's ancient inhabitants, the Canaanites. Once again, altars to Baal, Asherah and Moloch arose in the Promised Land. A brief summary of the taxing of God's patience is now in order. In the reigns of three kings (one of whom, Hezekiah, who essentially must be discounted), God has witnessed the alliance of his chosen nation with pagan powers, the wholesale, even enthusiastic adoption of Assyrian idol worship, human sacrifice offered by the king, the construction of a heathen altar in the Temple, the return to the original Canaanite heathen gods and the total rejection of His prophet Isaiah. Yet still God abides in the land, even yet He calls for repentance and continues to supply the prophetic message to the people of Judah. So, this is the presumed wrathful., even hateful God of the Old Testament?

As with much of the life itself of the prophet Isaiah the events of his demise cannot be stated with certainty, but that has not prevented centuries of speculation. The consensus belief is that he died early in the reign of King Manasseh and that further his death was that of a martyr. A Jewish and early Christian tradition maintains that Isaiah was the prophet who was "sawn asunder," literally cut in half, as described in the New Testament Book of Hebrews. In any event he passed from the scene and appeared to have no further influence on the nation of Judah. this is intrinsically believable inasmuch as his influence while living was minimal or non-existent. Kings and common people answered his prophetic exhortations with the sounds of silence. Well would Isaiah have often pondered that external question of man "What am I doing this for?"

A famous quotation from Shakespeare's "Julius Caesar" has Mark Antony orating to a multitude gathered to memorialize Caesar's death that:

"The bad that men do lives after them; The good is oft interred with their bones."

For once, the great poet may be wrong, and especially so in the case of Isaiah, a man who experienced little earthly payment or reward for his prodigious efforts. His good did not perish with him and in fact hundreds of years later as the sun rose upon the new dispensation of Christianity Isaiah's name, reputation and prophecy began to be understood and appreciated, so much that many have called Isaiah the Evangelist of the Old Testament. Arguably, even with his dearth of personal biographical information Isaiah is the Old Book's second most famous prophet (the most being the subject of a later essay). Doubtlessly, though, his prophecies are the most famous and most important revealed by the Old Testament. To some who measure only the moment Isaiah's life work may seem a disappointment. Seriously they may inquire how unheeded warning to kings and moral reprisals of the people can add up to great influence. It is not for these messages, these prophecies, though, in which Isaiah's memory and greatness are based. Rather it is setting forth beautifully and brilliantly the nature of the Promise which was to come seven centuries hence. Examined myopically and in an historical strait jacket the prophet's life appears of little effect. It is in that future, the future in which we all now dwell, that Isaiah's prophecy and God's patience come to fruition. Isaiah addressed his contemporaries in prophecies of events which lay in the distant future. None, absolutely none, of the persons whose ears may have heard his words understood their meaning. Almost of a certainty we may aver that it is unlikely that Isaiah himself grasped their entire meaning and importance. His book is filled with expressions which were baffling, as witness:

> "For this saith the Lord, Behold, I shall extend peace to (Jerusalem), and the glory of the Gentiles like a flowing stream..."

He included such prophecies of comfort as:

> "When the poor and needy seek water, and there is none... I the Lord will hear them, I the God of Israel will not forsake them"

Not all is comfort and softness from Isaiah's pen, for one will come, far greater than Isaiah who will be "despised and rejected of men." Yet even in the depths of degeneracy to which King Ahaz had plummeted, Isaiah offered the words which still thrill and give solace and hope to the believer:

> "Behold a virgin shall conceive, and bear a son, and shall call His name Immanuel."

Regretfully we must conclude that Isaiah received little positive recognition from his fellow citizens during his lifetime of prophecy. If we may employ such terms in describing the Divine it was a hard time for God, and His patience was stretched daily. Yet He knew and the believers of centuries to come know that while the great Isaiah lived in a time of war he was really prophesying of the coming of the Prince of Peace.

Chapter 6

MICAH: ONLY THE LONELY

*P*rophets were lonely souls. Most worked and prophesied if not in a vacuum, certainly in isolation from the mainstream of the day's culture, morals and thought. Working alone, though, does not necessarily equate to a type of moral segregation, of solitary confinement, for even at the times of lowest moral ebb the prophets had many (though far from a majority) of the Jewish people who stood with them. Much of the time the lonely prophet was not even the sole oracle of God, for often they had contemporaries who led separate existences but still proclaimed essentially the same message. Isaiah, of course, was one of the major prophets and figures of the Old Testament, but even he did not live his long-life absent voices who seconded his message. Of these perhaps the most prominent and perhaps the least read is a man named Micah, who in terms of prophetic span is an almost exact contemporary of Isaiah. A contemporary yes, but a duplicate no. Among the many talents of God is the Divine ability of supervision and management of people, a knowledge, found in very few persons, of assigning certain tasks to the right individuals, while simultaneously reserving other assignments for different persons. Whereas, Isaiah is most known for his prophecies and advice to kings and the even greater and more eternal Messianic prophecies, Micah's sphere was that of society itself. None of the components of the ancient nation of Judah (and to an extent that of Israel) passed from the prophet's gaze without his eyes and often his disapprobation falling upon them.

The scholars, academics and ordinary interests students of ancient history soon recognize an early confrontation that is theirs when they deal with ancient historical texts and accounts, and that is the relatively narrow lens through which the ancient historians, many of whose greatness is still not dimmed, viewed the world of which they wrote. The chronicles of ancient Greece and Rome, most well deserving of their historical reputation, focused primarily, if not at times even exclusively, upon the military and political stories of the nations of which they wrote. Battles, wars, the struggles of kings and queens, all received their due attention to the neglect of what today we reference as cultural, economic, and social matters. More plainly stated there exists a dearth of detailed accounts of the daily lives and difficulties of the ancients. Extant, though, is one glaring exception in the Holy Bible, among other attributes an account of how all, kings to commoners, saints and sinners, rich and poor, lived their daily lives, and it remains an invaluable treasure trove of information for us. All of which now brings us to one of the lesser known and celebrated prophets, Micah.

Micah lived, prophesied and wrote in an era in which enormous economic and social change had swept both Judah and Israel. Although primarily a messenger to the southern kingdom he did not neglect or except Israel from his teaching and prophecy. Earlier we saw that in the beginning of Isaiah's (and Micah's) careers as prophets Israel was facing enormous geopolitical pressure from the Assyrian Empire to the north, a pressure which eventually caused Israel to buckle and capitulate to this "people of the hooks," the Assyrians in 722 B.C. These prophecies had been wasted and squandered by the inhabitants of Israel, but time had not yet expired for Judah. This, though, was not the Judah of the days of David and Solomon, nor was it even the Judah of their successors. Through the generations Judah had grown more prosperous, life for many had become easier and more comfortable and these new realities alone brought change and social upheaval, most of it bad and morally disastrous to the Jews. Life was better for many, but they were benumbed to the reality and peril that they were living on the edge of survival and calamity and that the disaster that had befallen Israel could likewise happen to them. The crumbling and the disintegration of Judah's moral structure was not confined to any one group or social class, and therein lay much of the problem.

The growth and prosperity of Judah had given birth and rise to a condition which was anathema to God, and that is the development of social castes and classes. God had never had a desire for such among His people, and this factor alone exacerbated the moral decline of Judah. The prophet Micah took note, and he spoke and wrote. Here, now, the wellsprings and abundant depths of God's patience were not being tried merely by the folly and frivolity of Kings but by all across the social spectrum. Judah and especially the capital had become quite prosperous and with prosperity came inequalities and even inequities among the people. In short, some got very rich, while a larger contingent lived in grinding poverty. A central fact is best expressed here, although no time in history has this proposition been universally accepted. The rich are not inherently evil, nor are the poor necessarily virtuous. Both Testaments, including the message from Christ Himself is that riches are inherently dangerous and that service to them will result in moral corruption of the highest measure. So, it had become with ancient Judah. Micah's particular lot was that he had run afoul of many of the wealthy landowners, who by dishonest and/or overbearing methods were expropriating the lands and houses of the poorer. Placing it in the most human frame and image which may be invoked he declared that:

> "The women of my people have he cast out from their pleasant houses; from their children have ye taken away My glory forever."

The Gospels find Christ lashing such persons in His time as those that "...devour widows houses." A term often used today is "social justice", wording glaringly omitted from the Bible, which more plainly recognizes justice and injustice only. Social justice is a modern construct often deployed rhetorically in the vanguard of any political or social movement for the benefit of that particular cause. What Micah harshly condemns here is any person who utilizes an advantage to overwhelm and take from another. The wealthy more often possess such advantages, but it is the action that God condemns. This behavior in many forms and guises still is employed in all societies yet today. How remarkable is God's patience when He knows that the source of any person's riches is ultimately Himself. Yet oppression will always have its day in this world.

Wealth, riches, comfort and luxury may be the result of many things, proper timing, hard work, intelligent investing and even inheritance, and to the extent they are utilized for God the blessings of God are inherent and obvious. Money, or "filthy lucre" in the Biblically colorful phrase may also have its origins and roots not in the sunlit uplands of the world but rather in its poisoned sewers, and such was abundant in Judah. Jerusalem especially had been beautiful and brightened, and the Temple itself refurbished. Micah, though, did not count God among those who favored this because he plainly and publicly stated that most of the funds raised for this had come from the profit of prostitutes. Thus, ever has religion at times been based upon the most diseased and corrupt foundations. No more than a cursory glance at the New Testament will confirm this has often (sadly often) been a problem of those who have usurped Christianity for their private benefits and glories.

Yes, during Micah's life to an extent Judah remained religious, but of what value is religion alone? This study attempts to highlight the works, travails, tribulations and faith of prophets. Prophet, though, is not a synonym for truth and for good, and Micah's prophecy exposes the bad prophets, the bad religious leaders who exploit whomever and whatever they find, and in the phrasing of Peter in the New Testament "…make merchandise of you." During Micah's prophetic tenure in Judah, false prophets were thick on the ground. In the often-acerbic terminology of the prophets Micah spoke that

"…the prophets make my people err, they bite with their teeth, and cry, Peace."

False prophets, religious merchandisers and hucksters are not an invention of late twentieth and early twenty-first century American culture. The "televangelist" is new only in the sense that he has found great new tools with which to disseminate his underlying message of his own self-promotion. Only once in the New Testament did Christ act with violence towards anyone, and it was the Temple moneychangers who were the subjects of His anger and indignation. The same blasphemous attitude is found in the religious hierarchy and establishment of Micah's day. Even then God must have greatly coveted the concept of unleashing His anger, but rarely did He. Only God had the patience enough to withstand the mockery of His religion that His self-proclaimed religious leaders promulgated. Again, though His patience remained.

Although Isaiah was the prophet who dealt with the Kings of the day his contemporary Micah gave neither they nor their associates in the ruling and judicial classes any relief and surely no exoneration. Micah or anyone else merely had to look around to discern the moral state of Judah, and its people gave him a reading of the nature of their rulers. Of all the political systems devised by humanity, be they kingdoms, republics, democracies or dictatorships, few rarely escape a central truth that their rulers and leaders are rarely any better than the multitude of the populace whom they lead and rule. It is a pastime of the people of many nations in all ages to complain and bemoan the corruption of their leadership, the endless litany of the crimes and sins of their "crooked politicians." Rare is the person, especially in contemporary society who has not indulged and likely with an air or moral superiority in the excoriation of the political leaders of his day. The central truth, though, is that the moral standards of the political leadership rarely rise above the standards practiced by the population at large. The United Kingdom of Israel and Judah, for all its faults, once produced leaders of the caliber of Moses, David and Samuel, but now they were lacking. Although God recognized and even deplored the state of leadership, as much did He know that the mass of people themselves produced this moral quagmire. Still, even now through the reigns of terrible kings and the synthetic leadership of a dubious caste of priests God spared His wrath, exercised no vindictiveness and sent men such as Micah to help supply the comfort and balm of a spiritual solution. The patience of God is an awesome wonder.

The cultural corruption and rot had permeated deeply into Judah's society, and its burning acidic destruction was eating though the pillars of society. One of the marks of a stable, just and healthy society is a judicial or court system where every man and woman, no matter their status, could find impartiality and justice. This was to be a trademark, a touchstone even, of the nation which God had long ago brought from Egyptian slavery. Further unlike other ancient lands of this era Israel was given a highly detailed and articulated legal system for all its people, the Mosaical Law. They were certainly not lacking in a system of inherent equity and justice, a legal code designed by God Himself. Yet, all laws, even where the esteemed "Rule of Law" is most sacrosanct require humans to justly and fairly administer them. Micah, instead, surveyed the judges and judiciary of his day and found those that "...hate the good" and "eat the flesh of my people." Perhaps this is a more refined way of God's prophet articulating that the judges had effectively become "cannibals," feeding and even gorging off the people. Again, the wording seems to be a foreshadowing of the condemnation centuries later with which Christ lambasted the Pharisees that they "devour" widows' house and simultaneously make a pretense of their concern for the widows and orphans. A society which sees or even senses inequity and injustice in its system of adjudication leads its citizenry down paths of cynicism, distrust and ultimately in extreme instances, revolution. In Judah's case it also resulted in the vividly expressed revulsion of the system's Creator, but it did not lead to God's abandonment of His designs for Judah.

While God's patience is our central theme on the horizon now appeared both starkly and dimly but with ever powerful clarity the denouement of God's patience. Although Micah's life was lived in Judah and his prophecies directed primarily to his southern countrymen both God and the prophet were not unconcerned for the northern kingdom of Israel. In 722 B.C., during Micah's time of prophecy, the mighty Assyrians finally broke through and Israel became the empire's conquest. Gradually, over the years that followed most of the Israelites were enslaved, bound together as animals and forcibly removed from their homes to other lands in the Assyrian Empire. Gradually, they intermarried among the Gentiles, lost their identity as Israelites and Jews and became to history the fabled "ten lost tribes of Israel." They were not lost as much as assimilated into pagan Gentile culture, and the story of God's Chosen People, the Jews, would now be told solely through the southern Kingdom of Judah. This work shall shine its light upon Israel more directly and more thoroughly, but for now suffice it to say that Israel is no more. Through the eyes and teachings of His prophet Micah saw that

Judah, without massive reform, would see a similar end. Even after all, after centuries of misgovernment, rebellion and immorality God's deep reservoirs of patience with Judah were not yet drained.

The prophecies of Isaiah and Micah separately show but together are an overpowering indictment of the moral state of all levels of Judah's society. From kings, priests and judges to the ordinary man and woman morality's decline was apparent, and Judah's identity as a separate nation-state was fading. What, if anything could be done to reverse the descent into destruction? To the truly concerned it is never adequate to simply inventory the ills of a nation, shake one's head in despair perhaps tinged with a dollop of moral smugness, and simply walk away. It is incumbent upon the genuinely caring, those that truly care and even love the state or object of decline to at least suggest remedies which should be employed. Micah's authorship of his book was no private vanity enterprise but was rather inspired by God Himself. Micah moaned and lamented what he saw, but it was a sadness borne of his love for his fellow Jews.

So, the people and rulers of Judah needed to change, but change how and to what? It would indeed be a cruel God who decreed change but gave no indication of what the change should be. Here lies a central question, even a dilemma, which has been posed to mankind from the beginning of "what shall be?" Humanity still seeks, searches and gropes to correct and satisfying answers to this imposing question, and far flung are the fields in which he has sought the answer. Many enthusiasts, especially in the modern age have sought and even appeared certain that they had found all the answers in politics and political schemes. To vast hordes the answers lie in schemes such as communism, Nazism, fascism, socialism or perhaps even a special reverence for a monarch or a dictator. Even in ancient Biblical times people sought the answer in pleasure, the hedonistic lifestyle most succinctly expressed by a rich man in a parable of Christ, who spoke to his own soul with the gleeful admonition to "...take thine ease, eat drink and be merry."

Life's meaning and God's desires seem to be cavernously absent from any of these solutions. Further, only a fool would find life's meaning and answer in such cliched yet real dangers as sex, drugs or alcohol.

Where did God expect the Jews to turn at this critical juncture in their existence? An honest review compels us not to simply respond "religion," for religion itself has been and is at times as harmful as good. The religious establishment of Micah's day was corrupt, and in a different manner it was matched by the harshness and rigidity of the guardians of religion in Christ's time, of whom He spoke:

> "...(T)he people draweth to me with their mouth, and honoreth me with their lips; but their heart is far from me."

"Religion" per se is not nor has it ever been the right, or at least, not the entire answer to any human problem. In the Garden the first temptation of mankind was with the glitter of a religious incentive, that "...you shall be as gods." It was the religion of Egypt from which the Hebrews escaped, and it was the religion of the Canaanites and others of which God warned His followers never to go near.

The Lord did want His people to adopt religion, though, and it was a religion that once again He defined for them. Humanity has long studied its Creator and pondered His desires and designs for His creation. This study is known by many names, most commonly theology. It is through theology historically that mankind has made his greatest mistakes and errors in trying to understand God. Many persons, often well-meaning, have altered the structure of God's morality and His theology. David desired to construct a beautiful, elaborate Temple of worship, a Temple which he eventually if reluctantly allowed. Through Moses He provided a lengthy but essentially a simple law the moral principles of which are both proclaimed and summarized in the Ten Commandments. This was not enough for the religious "experts," though, for by the time of Christ they had added a vast library of men's traditions, both verbal and written to the Law. For this Christ harshly condemned them.

But back to the time of Micah and the precipitous decline of Judah. In passages in which Micah condemns not Judah but rather prays and pleads for its deliverance through God's mercy he speaks as the voice of God and expresses God's bewilderment with the people, a passage which justifies a lengthy quotation:

> "Oh my people, what have I done unto Thee? and
> wherein have I wearied thee? testify against me. For
> I have brought thee up out of the land of Egypt; and
> redeemed thee out of the house of servants."

God, who has been the victim of Judah's slights and its massive disregard for His ways is now the one who begs to understand the reasoning from this land of apostates. His patience has long passed the point of its evaporation for humans, but not for God. God wanted for them what He has always desired from His disciples, a love and devotion expressed in the deepest, but simplest terms. From the outset, man has sought to complicate what God has deemed to be simple, and from the beginning God's followers have battled, often literally, with themselves when it come to answering not just "Shall we follow God" but also "How shall we follow God."

When the prophet Micah deplored the lack of Judah's spirituality and its apostasy from God what did he propose in its stead. It is never enough to tell anyone just to "follow God" but rather it is also necessary to indicate the nature of the path that should be followed. Humanity designs elaborate theological structures, systems of religion. We are compelled to pose a question as incisive and relevant as it was in Micah's day and that is whether God is found in magnificently designed edifices and places of worship, in elaborate systems of carefully designed religion, in the division between the clerisy and the laity, catechisms and liturgies. Variants of this question were pondered in Micah's day, and the times both before and after. In the decades leading to the birth of Christ, a strikingly "religious" period in the Jew's history. Among many candidates and claimants two men in particular were recognized as the greatest scholars of the Jewish religion. They were contemporaries, and still known today their names were Shammai and Hillel. A prospective heathen student approached each man and requested that he be taught the entire law. Shammai passed on this, but Hillel answered:

> "What is hateful to you do not do to your neighbor;
> this is the entire Law, all the rest is commentary.
> Now go and learn it."

Later, during His short earthly ministry Christ was posed a similar question. Of course, the best answer to this query could have been supplied by no one but Christ, when He explained that the first and greatest commandment is to "...love the Lord thy God with all thy heart, and with all they soul, and with all thy mind.

And the second is like unto it, Thou shalt love they neighbor as thyself. On these two commandments hang all the law and the prophets."

Yet Micah too spoke eloquently on this subject. A long-suffering God's patience with Israel had after centuries expired, and the northern Kingdom had vanished. Judah was on the same fast track to destruction, and its demise appeared imminent. All God desired, though, were the fulfillment of the prophet's words in Micah's most famous verse:

"O man, what is good; and what doth the Lord require of thee, but to do justly, and to do mercy, and to walk humbly with thy God?"

How would Judah respond?

Chapter 7

ELIJAH: DID YOU EVER HAVE TO MAKE UP YOUR MIND?

*B*efore we continue with the developing story of Judah it is time that the gaze and concentration were focused upon those ten northern tribes which had seceded from the legitimate government and now constituted the separate kingdom of Israel. The division of the original nation was made in 931 BC with the succession of Jeroboam as the King of Israel, a man whose rule was unsuccessful and established a dreary pattern for all kings who followed him. Their names were Nadah, Baasha, Elah, Zimri, Tibni and Omri, and except for the last-mentioned king, all were cut from the same cloth. From what is known of them they were self-willed, self-absorbed, prone to immorality and a simple word understood by all-bad. Omri formed at best a partial exception, but this chapter is not his story so we will pass over him. To be fair this non-descript succession of non-entities had its hands full, for from 931 BC to 874 BC Israel had its share of problems, both foreign and domestic. The tiny kingdom was surrounded by hostile peoples, from Assyria and Syria to the north and east and its "brother"

Kingdom of Judah to the south. With these foes Israel waged almost continuous war, and with Assyria especially it was always in danger of being engulfed and destroyed.

Yet for all this the northern kingdom appeared to have achieved a certain tranquility and serenity in its daily existence and in the day-to-day mundane routine that composes so much of life. An agricultural land it appeared to have enjoyed a long run of development and prosperity and was seemingly very adept at adopting and assimilating foreign (i.e. Gentile) influences into its culture. Intermarriage of Jews with pagan Gentiles was becoming common and accepted, and its matrimonial path lightened by the man who in 872 BC became one of the most noteworthy monarchs' in the entire Bible, King Ahab. So exactly who was Ahab? In that wonderfully succinct and descriptive way the Bible has with words let us quote his introduction:

> "And Ahab the son of Omri did evil in the sight of the
> Lord above all that were before him."

What a thematic phrase by which to debut, and as we shall see King Ahab lived up to this description. Ahab was no fool, and he seems to have been an intelligent and, in many ways, a highly capable man. He possessed leadership skills as a military commander on the field of battle was a brave man and took his role and responsibility seriously. Yet, all in all, though, he would demonstrate that in addition to his moral defects he was an inherently weak man. Seeking to cement an alliance (in which he was successful) with Israel's northern neighbor, a Canaanite power known as Phoenicia, Ahab took as his queen a Phoenician princess whose name almost three thousand years hence remains synonymous with feminine wiles and evil, Jezebel. This monarch (in name and in attitude) was not just a Gentile with Gentile religion, but she was more, a fanatical pagan, who sought to eradicate the God of Israel from Israel itself.

Once again, though, let us look at the land itself and its inhabitants and try to achieve some illumination on what it must have been to live in Israel during the early reign of Ahab and Jezebel. Degrees in history or sociology are not requisite for any to make the observation that whether it be the ancient or modern world, be it the East or the West, of whatever race or nationality most people desire a reasonable amount of stability in their lives, so that their daily existence is not a haphazard lottery in which anything is liable to happen. Let us grant a fair allocation of praise to Ahab and Jezebel, for their strong rule was providing a solid backdrop and an existence upon which the "average" Israelite could count and rely upon many things. With the coming of Jezebel came the full panoply of Canaanite gods, and an Israelite could count upon seeing their idols wherever he gazed, and the foremost among them was Baal, the god of human sexuality and fertility. Where once stood places of worship to the God of Israel altars and temples to Baal and his fellow Canaanite gods and goddesses were being erected. An Israelite could now rely upon a massive and overwhelming influx of Canaanite "morality" and pagan degeneracy. Temple prostitution, a common mark of heathen religion, became a common money-making device of religion .

An Israelite could now depend upon the absence of the great leaders of Israel's past, men and women such as Moses, Joshua, Deborah, Samuel and David, persons and leaders who advanced God's designs. Instead he could count upon his present King Ahab to be prominent in the advance of his wife's aggression in making the Canaanite religion that of Israel. The common man or woman could rely upon the increasing glorification of heathen thinking and morality, and the increasing intolerance and outright persecution of those few who were known to cling to the Israelite religious rites and practices, which were being subjected to increasingly rapid and far-flung changes. Rather than the priesthood and priests ordained by God in the Book of Leviticus she would be aware of the increasing prominence and power of priests who served gods with strange names such as not only Baal but the likes of Asherah and Moloch. The ancient Israelites, be they king or commoner, failed to count on one central and salient fact, and that was God's ability to raise up a man such as Elijah.

He is introduced to us as Elijah the Tishbite, and there the questions begin. Three millennia have not provided sufficient time for scholars to agree on the location of the Tishbites, although a consensus seems to have formed that it was in the land of Gilead, east of the Jordan River. Nothing is known of his ancestry, his looks or his age, though here again it is asserted that he was a young man, perhaps in his early thirties when he makes his first appearance. He is the most famous of all the Old Testament prophets, though this is strange when we consider that he wrote not a single word of prophecy. Only God ultimately determines the importance of lives, but it may be asserted that Elijah's prophecy was not the most important, that niche occupied by Isaiah, who prophesied so much about the coming Messiah and the dawn of Christianity. Elijah, though, may rightfully claim the honors as the most "spectacular" of the prophets, and likely of any person in the Old Testament. So much of Elijah's life is played on a dramatic stage that almost compels the attention of the spectator, believer and unbeliever alike. Moreover, he is the man whose name became almost synonymous with the term "prophet" and along with Moses one of the two greatest figures in Israel's spiritual history.

For the present purposes both Elijah as a man and a prophet along with the prophet's deeds can rightfully assert claim as the fullest and greatest example of God's patience exhibited through the life of a single man. Further it is no trivialization of either God's designs or Elijah as a man to say that he is reminiscent of the classic hero of fiction, perhaps found in its purest form in American westerns, the man of unknown background, of somewhat mysterious origins who suddenly appears for a time, performs feats of courage, justice and heroism and then moves on. This is Elijah.

Elijah's first pronouncement is of dramatic splendor, when he confronts Ahab and proclaims:

> "As the Lord God of Israel liveth, before whom I stand, there shall not be dew nor rain these years..."

To a modern Western urbanized and suburbanized society, a drought can pose difficulties. Lack of moisture becomes uncomfortable, outdoor activities are curtailed and prices of food and water rise. To an ancient primitive agriculturally based economy such as Israel prolonged drought equated to suffering, illness and death, often on a massive scale. Suffice it to observe it would obtain the attention of everyone. For three long years does this drought remain, and the suffering is intense. It also gives the backdrop for one of the most famous narratives regarding animals, once known by all Sunday School children, Elijah's being miraculously fed by the ravens. Ahab, though was not interested in Sunday School stories, but rather the end of the drought of terror and the destruction of the prophet. Nonetheless, Ahab was humbled enough that he went to see Elijah, a meeting which would showcase one of history's greatest exchanges of dialogue. Upon seeing Elijah, the King exclaimed: "Art thou he that troubleth Israel?"

The great prophet, though, responded with devastation: " I have not troubled Israel but thou, in that ye have forsaken the commandments of the Lord, and thou hast followed Baal."

This exchange, though, would not amount merely to verbal sparring, for Elijah issued a challenge whose drama would play on Mount Carmel, and with the earlier parting of the Red Sea, perhaps one of the two most spectacular Old Testament scenes. Effectively, Elijah challenged both Ahab and the Israelite people to a "showdown." To the Israelite people Elijah issued a challenge, a question to which every person who ever lived must give an answer:

"How long halt ye between two opinions? if the Lord be God, follow him: but if Baal, follow him. And the people answered not a word."

It was a portentous question, and it fairly exuded God's growing impatience with the Israelite people. Through his prophet Elijah He would supply them more reason to answer God rather than Baal.

The great god Baal had already daily and dramatically failed the Israelites. He, we remember, was the god of fertility, but not just human sexual fertility. In the pantheon of Canaanite deities, he was the god who supplied the rain which grew crops from the now fertile ground. For three years Baal had proven to be a spectacular failure, as the parched earth gave little or nothing, and the populace was starving. God would give Baal one more chance, a public dramatic chance to brandish his credentials and prove his nettle as a fertility god, a deity who could draw rain from the heavens.

On the strictest of numerical terms, the odds against God and Elijah were 850 to one, for on Carmel that date the God of Israel, the God who had centuries ago emancipated their ancestors from Egyptian slavery and given them law and freedom was represented by the lone figure of Elijah. The Canaanite deities had four hundred prophets of Baal and four hundred fifty devoted to the goddess Asherah, the cult-deity of wooden idols. The contest was to be dramatic, yet in actuality quite simple, and its goal was nothing more nor less than to determine who was "God in Israel." Two bullocks for sacrifice were to be taken, one for each side, each to be prepared and laid on the wood of a sacrificial altar but the wood to be unified. The deities themselves would be summoned to provide the fire.

Since Elijah was the host (and also likely aware of the immense dramatic possibilities of going second) he graciously offered center stage and the opportunity to draw first blood to the worshippers of

Baal. Diligently did these Canaanite clerics prepare the bullock and altar for the great sacrifice to Baal. All were now to be treated to pagan worship practices and rituals in their full dramatic splendor. Early in the morning did the supplications to Baal commence, with literally hundreds of his prophets together in unison swaying back and forth, bending their knees and hopping on one foot like children playing. Often the greatest satirical parodies are self-parodies, and it is hard not to see such with the Baalite prophets hopping and bouncing around in self-mockery and unconscious agreement with Elijah that they were "halt" and thus limping along in the Canaanite religion. Still nothing happened, and from morning to early evening the prophets of Baal expended copious quantities of energy and received nothing in return. At some human level, though, even a believing Christian must acknowledge, if not exactly, admire their commitment and sincerity. The holy men of Baal had taken their offering to a different level, but by a method not unknown even to certain pagan cults yet today. In the gruesome language they began to engage in self-flagellation:

> "And they cried aloud, and cut themselves with knives and lancets, till the blood gushed about them"

Such was their frenzy that the behavior of many became self-destructive, but still to no avail. By the time of the intended offering of the evening sacrifice nothing had happened, truly nothing. No response, no answer and no noise whatsoever came from Baal or any Canaanite deity. The maniacal efforts of hundreds of priests and prophets caused not a divine stir, and the god of rain and fertility provided nothing.

During the hours of the Canaanite catastrophe it is undeniable that the opposition, the lonely man Elijah, was enjoying himself. Actually, though, the mundane phrase "enjoying himself" is really too bland and non-descriptive. Elijah was "having fun," an incongruous behavior we seldom associate with or attribute to the supposedly stern and sober Old Testament prophets. By noon Elijah was fully aware that the Canaanite priests were adrift on a sea of futility:

> "An it came to pass at noon, that Elijah mocked them, and said Cry aloud: or he is a god; either he is talking, or he is pursuing, or he is in a journey, or peradventure he sleepeth, and must be awakened."

Those are the words of a man who is keenly aware that it is not enough to say that the odds were heavily in his favor, for there was nothing of the wager in this contest. Elijah had known with certainty that this would occur, and just as surely was he cognizant of the fulfillment of the next age in this contest and drama. Baal's section of the two-act show was an abysmal failure, and the attention of the multitudes began to turn towards Elijah.

Elijah's God, though, was not and never will solely be a God of words alone, but also of action. Carmel was apparently chosen for this drama because there lay an old altar to God, broken and in disrepair, which Elijah then had reconstructed. He had twelve stones utilized, the twelve symbolizing the true twelve tribes of a united Israel, not this rump Kingdom ruled by Ahab. The altar, rebuilt and refurbished, was to serve as the traditional place of animal sacrifice. Upon the altar the sacrificial bullock was lain, but Elijah ordered more to come. Not according to custom, he directed a deep trench to be dug around the altar. The he strangely decreed that not once, not twice, but three times was the altar and sacrifice to be drenched with water and the trench similarly filled to capacity.

Now in the shade of the evening and likely with the full attention of the crowd Elijah turned his eyes heavenward and beseeched:

> "Lord God of Abraham, Isaac and of Israel, let it be known this day that thou art God in Israel, and

that I am thy servant, and that I have done all these things at thy word."

Both then and now God, this time though His great prophet Elijah, knew how to build a story until it crescendos to its dramatic peak. With this God's fire fell, and not only consumed the animal sacrifice, but also the stone altar, the wood and the water in the trench. Baal, his fellow gods and goddesses, and the priests who, in those magnificently descriptive Old Testament words "fed at Jezebel's table" were crushed, an overwhelming, overpowering defeat. God was not yet through with them, though. He had seen ten of the tribes which He brought from Egyptian slavery rebel and form their own secessionist government of Israel. God had patiently endured one wretchedly horrible king after another, and seen Canaanite idolatry, against which He had warned Israel the entire tenure of its existence, and overtly He had done nothing. this was a God of almost infinite patience, but here the patience failed Him. Now, the Israelites on Mount Carmel, suddenly electrified by a surge of religion, heeded Elijah's dictate that the apostate prophets of Baal be taken down to the banks of the brook Kishon, where they were executed. Evidently, God's patience, far-reaching and more forgiving than the patience of any of His creation had shown one of its limitations. For the Israelites and their religious elite had spurned the first of the Commandments which God had given to Moses: "I am the Lord thy God... Thou shalt have no other gods before me."

Perhaps too we should consider that in addition to being the universe's Creator and Ruler God is also possessed of a personality, a personality that was shown beautifully in the character of His son, Jesus Christ. The northern kingdom was borne of an illegitimate king and his successors were no better, often worse, and the kingdom had sunk to a morass of the most deplorable heathen practices. The priests of Baal were the sycophants of the queen and scripturally identified as parasites. God was fully justified in executing the consequences upon a depraved group.

The story has not reached its ultimate chapter, for it must be remembered that this dramatic climax on Carmel had grown from the effects of a drought begun three years earlier. The god of Baal could deliver no rain, but the God of Israel could. Elijah told King Ahab that the rain was coming in abundance and that Ahab should return to his home in Jezreel before the parched earth became impassable mud. Elijah, doubtless still excited and with the advantages of youth and God arrived in Jezreel before Ahab with the news of Baal's rout and obviously the ending of the drought.

Were the Old Testament a work of fiction it is likely that the story of Elijah's public career in prophecy would now close. A spectacular triumph had been secured in a dramatic superlative manner, the pagan priesthood destroyed, the reprobate king reproved and humiliated, and most importantly the people knew the identity of God in Israel. Surely there would now occur a revival of the spirit in the populace and the population would return enmasse to God and rebuild the spiritual structure and strength of the nation. A marvelous story in would have been, but instead – absolutely nothing happened, and nothing changed. Still, one person changed or perhaps it would be better stated that she found a resolve that had heretofore gone unexpressed. Queen Jezebel announced that within twenty-four hours the prophet Elijah would be as the prophets of Baal, that is dead. Quickly Elijah fled Jezreel and with God's help made a desperate journey through the Sinai Desert to the "mountain of God," otherwise known as Mt. Horeb or Mt. Sinai, a place of some historical significance. Here, a weary fugitive, the despairing Elijah would meet both his fate and his God. What would it be?

Chapter 8

ELIJAH: ALL ALONE AM I

*I*t has many sides and facets and goes by many names, only a few of which are sadness, loneliness, despair, despondency, the "blues" melancholy, etc., but its catchall term, the most encompassing and the one which instantly leaps out at the human psyche is the one most commonly employed-depression. How tempting it is to assert that almost all human beings of all ages have suffered from its dark shadows, but unfortunately that itself is too tepid a statement. So, we state without equivocation that all of earth's mortals have met it, dreaded its spectre, and generally survived, although not without wounds and scars. Neither are Old Testament heroes and prophets exempt from its tortures, and this included, perhaps with special lessons, the most famous of these prophets, Elijah.

A predecessor and his equal in fame and later veneration was Moses, who certainly partook from a veritable feast of troubles during his lifetime. Moses, though, after his epic battles with Pharaoh, was given the burden but the glory of leading the Hebrews from Egypt and establishing a new nation. In contrast, Elijah utterly routed the Canaanites upon Mount Carmel and doubtless well expected this to be the starting nexus of Israel's great spiritual revival. Instead, the effect of its splendor quickly was extinguished, and Elijah, a condemned man, had fled through the desert to the presumed safety and certain loneliness of Mt. Horeb. Here, in the despondency of his soul so dark he saw nothing but loneliness and impending doom and requested that God proceed and take his life. From this darkness which was slowly enveloping the prophet a man already great, would emerge and become a synonym and a byword for spiritual strength and splendor. Of equal and likely importance, the depths of God's love and patience with his own disciples would truly shine.

Let us employ strikingly modern terminology and emphatically state that Elijah "had a right" to be depressed. He had done everything for which God had commissioned him, his success was awe-inspiring and publicized throughout the land and now he was left alone, literally having lived in a cave for forty nights, with a fanatical woman, intoxicated by power and self-importance, having sworn his death. Elijah, too, was consuming that devil's food of depression, the morose realization of being all alone, so much so that in defending his behavior to God he exclaimed that "...I, even I only, am left; and they seek my life, to take it away." This was part of the rehearsal of his discourse to God, explaining to Him what the Lord already knew all too well. Yet, God let Elijah have his say, and let him speak without interruption and withheld telling him those dread words that friends and loved ones will often sincerely offer that "...you should not feel that way." Especially in the complex, modern world do persons often need particular mental and emotional help, be it from a psychiatrist, a psychologist, a counselor or just a close confidante. In the foundation of help, though, the reserves offered to the patient seem to have a commonality, and it appears that God drew heavily upon these reserves of care, understanding and patience to help Elijah.

First of all, He gave to Elijah that precious commodity of time in which to recover. Here at Mt. Horeb he had fed and succored Elijah for some forty days, well over a month to recover from the trauma. God offered no condemnation, no chastisement and no words of rebuke to Elijah. Rather, he reminded Elijah that even the great prophet would not participate in or view a life of dramatic scenes, of fires, earthquakes, gales and storms but rather even he would sense God in the quietness, in the peace and serenity of life and in His words to "...still, small voice."

Then God was highly sensitive to the realization that His great, vigorous and dynamic prophet needed work, work in which his natural energies and sense of service would flourish. Then, return to Israel by way of Damascus, for there Elijah was to anoint a man named Hazael as the next King of Syria. More importantly God above all knew that Ahab would not be King forever, and Elijah was to anoint John as his successor. Of the greatest substance, though, Elijah was to meet a man whom God had chosen as Elijah's own successor, a man whose fame and prowess would be little short of Elijah's.

In a closing word to this scene in Elijah's life God answers Elijah's assertion of loneliness, that he was the only follower of Israel's God remaining in Israel. No, in words and a thought that resounds yet today he bolstered the prophet by relating that:

> "I have left me seven thousand in Israel, all the knees
> which have not bowed unto Baal, and every mouth
> which hath not kissed him."

Any reasonably intelligent person should halt before uttering a statement such as "Things are not as bad as they seem," for we know that life guides us, unfortunately but so, to a realization that matters may be as bad or even worse than what they seem. It may be boldly asserted, however, that matters "usually" are not as bad as they appear, and often appreciably better. What a counselor God has been to Elijah, and how exemplary it abides as a lesson for us. A despairing and despondent Elijah was given those items which are vital, even requisite, to the psychological and spiritually depressed. He was given adequate time to recover, to take stock of his situation, and yes, even to "bleed" a little before the recovery could really commence. He was neither condemned nor berated for his feelings and most decidedly was not told that he was feeling sorry for himself. How important it is for all of us, including such a great figure, to be free to express the deepest feelings and emotions cannot be overrated. Likely most important of all he was given important work to accomplish and a renewed sense of purpose. Although the Bible is not a psychiatric text, it might be a hopeless endeavor to discover a better pattern and template to follow whenever we experience the downs, the troughs and the depressions, which are an inevitable element in the lives of all, including believing Christians.

Besides the tasks here assigned what else lay ahead for the prophet? Were the moments of great drama and spectacular deeds relegated to reminiscences? King Ahab still ruled Israel, and for all his faults he was not a king totally bereft of accomplishments. At war and as a military leader King Ahab excelled, and he soon led Israel's army to a victory in a war against the King of Syria. Exhibiting the skills, experience and foresight of an adroit king and general he fortified Israel's cities which lay along the Syrian border. Well done we should say, but praise and credit given to this king should be meted out sparingly. Military prowess, skills and accomplishments are sometimes essential for a nation's survival, but history's roster of military greats includes a great host of men with names such as Julius Caesar, Genghis Khan and Napoleon Bonaparte, none of whom would be moral exemplars to any but their most fanatical devotees. Ahab's heart and intentions remained as black as coal.

From creation forward most of humanity has desired to live as well as possible, and it is common to all to which for an abundance of these things in life which give us pleasure. Kings and queens especially seem to be endowed with these traits. From his wars with Syria (where incidentally he had displeased God) King Ahab returned to his home in Samaria. Adjacent to his royal palace in Jezreel was a fine tract of land coveted by Ahab as a garden for herbs. He thus entered into negotiations with the owner of the parcel, a man named Naboth, who was using the land as a vineyard. Ahab, a man and a king who had developed a well-deserved reputation for harsh and spiteful conduct, appeared remarkably reasonable in his approach to Naboth. In exchange for the land Ahab offered him "a better vineyard" or if he so desired, its worth in money. Naboth, though, was in no mood to bargain and rejected Ahab by advising the King he felt a sacred obligation to retain the land because it was an inheritance from his forefathers:

To state that Ahab did not take this rejection well is to utter an understatement of Biblical proportions. Spurned by the intransigency of one of his subjects Ahab returned home, and his behavior requires a scriptural quotation:

> "And Ahab come into his house heavy and displeased because of the word which Naboth the Jezreelite had spoken to him: for he had said, I will not give thee the inheritance of my fathers. And he laid down upon his bed, and turned away his face, and would eat no bread."

The great king of Israel, a military commander of demonstrated ability, a monarch whose word and even his disapproving glance feared, doubtless a real "man's man" has assumed the role of petulant young teenager (boy or girl) whose great quest for love and approval has been rejected. He literally throws himself on his bed, turns to the wall and refuses to eat, a true testament to his character and leadership. Earlier we reflected that Ahab's heart was as black as coal, but this is an assertion subject to qualitative comparison. King Ahab was many evils wrapped in the person of one man, but every fiber of his moral character was not uniformly deplorable. His sins were as scarlet, yet he remained at some level an Israelite and an Israelite King.

Though he came of age in an evil time Ahab was not unfamiliar with concepts such as individual rights, private property and in general the rule of law. In his administration, however, he simply ignored much of this. With an initial apparent good fortune Naboth was to be the beneficiary of Ahab's impulse to abide by the law and respect Naboth's refusal to part with his vineyard. The impulse, though, was quickly channeled into another, quite infamous stream of action, and the captain of this cruise was Queen Jezebel. The names Ahab and Jezebel to this day are inextricably linked and intertwined. Their reign was wicked and ignoble, but they remained two separate individuals. In the wardrobe of wickedness Jezebel well supplied those few garments which Ahab was missing. These quaint, old-fashioned notions of laws and rights belonged to a primitive, outdated societal model such as Israel. She had the royal lineage of a Canaanite princess, and in her worldview the desires, even the whims of kings and queens were there to be satisfied.

So, Jezebel approached her prostrate husband and queried why he was so glum, and Ahab responded with his woeful tale of being refused his coveted vineyard. Jezebel, too, had a response, one that has been employed by kings, emperors, presidents on down to all manner of petty tyrants from time immemorial. You, my dear husband, are king and you, not a nobody such as Naboth rules Israel. More succinctly stated, "You have the power. Use it!" Ahab may have possessed the power, but it was Jezebel who was the owner of the rich, scheming brilliance which she now zestfully employed to "...let thine heart be merry (for) I will give you the vineyard of Naboth the Jezreelite." Disregarding the moral revulsion and sheer repugnance of the plan Jezebel's plotted maneuverings are those of a master.

The Queen of Israel proceeded to forge letters in the King's name (complete with the king's royal seal) and they were dispatched to the scattered leaders in the land. The letters were exemplary of the modern scourge of micro-managing at its worst. A fast was to be proclaimed throughout Israel, not an unusual event in this ancient society, and the attention of the multitudes of observants was to be fixed on Naboth by placing his "on high" or in the center of the proceedings. Then demonstrating that lack of moral scruples which centuries after reached its pinnacle in the trial of Christ they were further instructed to:

> "...set two men, sons of Belial, before him, to bear witness against him, saying, Thou didst blaspheme God and the king, And then carry him out, and stone him, that he may die."

As later the conspirators against Christ knew so well, when all else fails – Lie. Again, that wonderfully descriptive language of the Bible, here "sons of Belial" which can also be translated as "worthless men" an acutely accurate description of the perjuring witnesses. Oftentimes the worst, the most sinister and foul plots work, and so did this one, exactly as planned. If Ahab's heart was black as coal, then Jezebel's was as hard as stone. Evil did not really penetrate the heart of Jezebel, for rather the reverse is true. Evil pulsated and radiated from that black rock, wherein others have some measure of heart and feelings.

Life seemed to be good for the royal couple with all enemies, whether foreign or domestic, either vanquished or quiet. They lived in a palace in a prosperous nation , had apparently absolute power, and Jezebel had demonstrated that she had an apparent magic touch that could aggrandize their wealth and appetites at any moment. Even the smartest, most cunning and most diabolical of villains make mistakes, and sometimes they make the same mistake twice. Earlier our attention was drawn to the condition of Israel and how that with the advent and development of Ahab's reign the Israelite people could count on many certainties. In their snug secularizion they had overlooked one item which then loomed large and was about to do so again. God is always an observer of human affairs, then and now, and sometimes He even elects to be a participant. Yet again, "...the word of the Lord cam to Elijah the Tishbite" whom God called upon once again to confront King Ahab. God then ordained a prophetic certainty, a fact of an almost ghoulish quality to Ahab the murderer:

> "And thou shalt speak unto Him, saying, Thus saith
> the Lord, Hast thou killed, and also taken possession"

This was the verdict, and the sentence followed:

> "Thus saith the Lord, in the place where dogs lick
> the blood of Naboth shall dogs lick thy blood, even
> thine."

Further the effects of Ahab's deeds would live after him, for Ahab was informed that his family dynasty was finished because he had "... provoked me to anger and made Israel to sin."

Jezebel, the prime mover behind Naboth's murder and so many of Ahab's nefarious activities was herself in no manner ignored or spared. Most of the wives of Israel's kings were queens by way of marriage only and left the actual roles of governing to the ordained king, but certainly not so with Jezebel. It is too tepid and ineffective to merely state that Jezebel was the "power behind the throne" for often she was the throne itself, a fact hardly unnoticed by God as witness Elijah's prophecy and condemnation: "The dogs shall eat Jezebel by the walls of Jezreel."

Kings and queens are unaccustomed to having anyone, let alone their perceived enemy Elijah, saying such words to them face-to-face. Each would suffer the indignities of being consumed by dogs upon their deaths, so a word about the dogs is advisable. In the modern world we think of dogs as pets, and they are rightfully beloved to vast numbers of enthusiasts. They share our hearths, homes and hearts and deservedly so. The ancient societies more often viewed them as unclean, effectively scavengers who loved beyond the pale of societal acceptance, and doubtless Ahab and Jezebel processed these prophecies of doom in this light. Strangely, Elijah's prophecies to the royal duo each omitted one salient fact, and that was time. When were these morbid fates to occur, tomorrow, or next year or in the distant future? Ahab and Jezebel were now to witness and to live with God's patience for many years to come, through changing seasons, new faces and ever changing personal and political scenes.

As the years rolled by Israel's political situation and at times its very existence was continually under siege usually from the north and customarily against Syria. Towards the end of his reign Ahab had allied Israel with its brother kingdom to the south, Judah, and both fought Syria at Rameth-gilead. In the action as always, Ahab disguised himself as an ordinary soldier on the battlefield. A Syrian archer's arrow struck him between the joints of his armor, and Ahab's life ended later that evening. It was a bloody wound which the king suffered, and its streams spread about on the chariot on which Ahab was riding. The Israelites returned to Samaria, and in the aftermath of the battle and Ahab's death:

> "...one washed the chariot in the pool of Samaria;
> and the dogs licked up his blood ... according to the
> word of the Lord which he spake."

The death of a king rarely ends the life of a nation, and it was with Israel. The office experienced no vacancy, for Ahab's son Ahaziah quickly took his father's place and quickly demonstrated that he was a worthy successor to his father, Ahab, for it was immediately established that he, too, would be a Baal worshiper. Quickly he ran afoul of Elijah, and just as quickly did the reign of Ahaziah cease after only one year. At Ahaziah's death, the monarchial throne was assumed by his brother Jehoram for perhaps twelve years, although its exact tenure is historically uncertain. Through all this Jezebel survived and perhaps no longer at the center of matters her influence, her presence and shadow loomed large. Effectively, Israel was now more Canaanite than it was Israel.

Jehoram's reign seemed to brew discontent, and finally his own army rose in rebellion. Led by an officer named Jehu the soldiers killed the King Jehoram as he attempted to escape to the presumed safe haven of Jezreel. Jehu pressed on to Jezreel, and the news of his coming preceded him, reaching the ears of the queen, who planned one last dramatic scene in her life of royal splendor. She attired herself in queenly splendor, "painted her face" in the words of the scriptures, adorned her hair and taunted Jehu from her palace window as he led his troops into Jezreel. No dramatic death scene, no Hollywood-style execution was to be allowed the once all-powerful princess. Jehu ordered that she be thrown from the palace window. Her servants (likely with a lightness of heart) threw her from the window, the queen ricocheted from the palace walls, sprinkling with blood, and her body trampled by the soldiers' horses as they rode over it. When the burial detail was later sent to tend to its trash the men returned and reported to Jehu that it had found no more of the queen than her skull, feet and the palms of her hands. Jehu recalled Elijah's prophecy of a quarter century earlier that in Jezreel would "… dogs eat the flesh of Jezebel." As icing on the royal cake he directed that whatever remained of be unburied and as "…dung upon the face of the field in Jezreel."

Naboth's death had been the news of a previous generation, as he lay dead and buried for twenty-five years. The miracle of Mount Carmel was likely a memory of only a few faithful souls, and even Ahab was gone. Elijah had been swept away by God and immortalized in memory, scripture and reality. Only Jezebel remained. And God with His promise of her macabre death scene.

The epic tale of Elijah's life and prophecy's is perhaps the fullest, most complete review and showcase in the entire Old Testament for God's patience. For this truncated kingdom of ten secessionist tribes to have even survived until the days of Elijah is a marvel, and in the most literal sense could have been achieved only through the patient grace of God. It is a marvel that God's patience and tolerance did not crumble after the miraculous intervention on Mount Carmel. All dazzling offering of God's power was answered by the inertia of the Israelite people, still holding to its basic course of idolatry.

For the Christian, though, the most illustrative and in one instance comforting demonstrations of God's patience are shown in two matters. Ahab and Jezebel, forever linked as a couple and as mighty examples of rebellion, blasphemy and abuse of power, met their dooms not immediately, but years, and in Jezebel's case, a generation later. As the Bible records God is "not slack in His promises" even when the promise's fulfillment is not pleasant. It is with Elijah himself, though, that God's message of patience, understanding and solace for the Christian and to which the Christian looks as a guide to conduct. The prophet was devastated when the miracle's effects seemed to count for nothing and instead, he became a fugitive and a target for royal murder. He ran from the problem and quite plainly felt sorry for himself. Yet who would not, and so did God understand His great and beloved messenger. God demonstrated Divine love and patience, and soon Elijah was back in the fray, as great as ever.

With the Genesis figure of Enoch, Elijah is known as one of only two men taken directly to heaven. Gone for a very long time His memory and legacy began to grow among the Israelites of a later time to a point where he became in retrospect, along with Moses, one of the nation's two greatest spiritual leaders. A moment in the first century AD in Caesarea Philippi found Christ standing surrounded by the heathen stone idols of the Gentiles. He was accompanied by His apostles and He asked them a question to which

James Kifer

He received numerous answers. Simply the question was "Whom do men say that I the son of marram?" Among those answers was "Elijah" a prophet so powerful and great that many took him for the very Messiah Himself.

Chapter 9

ELISHA CURES NAAMAN - YOU'RE SO VAIN

*W*e have coined many phrases and repeatedly employed them all to describe a situation that presents inherent difficulties for any individual. They include "He's a tough act to follow," "I would not want to be in your shoes" or more derogatorily "he is a pale imitation" of his predecessors. These are ways of recognizing an elemental human difficulty in succeeding a man or woman who has been so famous and adept in performing their tasks that the minds of most will automatically establish them as the standard to which all are compared, and certainly this is especially and notoriously true for their immediate successors. The historical and political scenes provide an almost endless array of examples that may be cited. American history causes us to invoke the names of certain presidents who have become in retrospect quasi-religious figures in the estimation of many. Yet who but a student of history can quickly supply the names of the successors to George Washington and Abraham Lincoln? Certainly, the Bible is not lacking in questions, answers and problems of succession to great men and women. Many of the successors of the great lived lives of abysmal failure, and quickly King Solomon flashes to mind. A man of enormous gifts and blessings he was the son and successor of the man to this day is recognized as Israel's greatest leader, King David. Samuel, likely the greatest and most important of the judges lived the heartache and pain of watching his two sons, Hophire and Phineas, become synonymous with bribery and criminal chicanery as judges.

But not all successors of the great went the way of the world. Moses, proclaimed Israel's great Deliverer and spiritual leader, was synonymous with strength and leadership for four decades. Who could with any success step from his shadow and fulfill this role? God was not lacking, for he had Joshua, a wise seasoned leader and expert military commander and strategist. The question before God and the northern kingdom of Israel was, at this moment, who could possibly take Elijah's place? Unsurprisingly God had found his man and found him while Elijah was alive and on this earth.

Our narrative now recalls from memory that the depression of Elijah after the contest on Mount Carmel was succeeded by Jezebel's pledging his death. After the forty days and nights at Mt. Horeb, God recalled Elijah to duty and an awareness of his great obligation. He was to arise, and among other matters, go and anoint a man named Elisha to be his successor. So forward Elijah went and came to this man, described as the son of Shamhat, and found him plowing a field. Elisha, though, was no ordinary farm boy or plowman, for he was plowing not just with a single ox but with eleven more worked by servants to him. In this ancient agricultural land those were indicia of wealth, making Elisha a man of substance and reputation. The initial meeting of the two prophets has provided the world with an example not entirely outmoded even today when describing the transference of power, authority and responsibility. Elijah passed by Elisha and "cast his mantle upon him," signifying that was the great prophet's successor. No doubt it was a startled Elisha who merely requested time to return to his mother and father to kiss them goodbye. The Christian instantly calls to mind the words of Christ, spoken centuries later:

"No man, having put his hand to the plow, and looking back is fit for the Kingdom of God."

Was Elisha such a man, and was God's patience with his chosen servant to be immediately extinguished? The answers are emphatically no, for while Elisha surely loved his home and parents, his commitment to God was foremost in his thinking and his life. When his soon-to-be mentor seemingly to display a lack of enthusiasm for Elisha's suggested homecoming Elisha proved his mettle as a committed prophet by taking a yoke of his oxen and used them for the basis of a feast soon enjoyed by the poor of the area. Although he was wealthy, he now embarked on a storied career as not only God's but in a manner of speaking the "people's prophet". From the silence of the scripture, however, apparently Elisha remained in an apprenticing role for several years, as Elijah holds center stage for some time to come. Elisha, by name, reappears in a memorable scene at Elijah's departure.

Elijah, about to depart from this world, crossed the Jordan River, and Elisha insisted upon giving with the reluctant Elijah. Elisha asked Elijah for a "double share of your spirit" and so it was granted, contingent upon Elisha's lifelong faithfulness. Elijah, as great a Biblical figure as any, was miraculously swept heavenward on a "chariot of fire" becoming one of only two mortals to never taste death.

He was now indisputably God's prophet on earth, and Elisha's primary concern remained his own countrymen, the Israelites of the northern kingdom. Unlike Elijah, though, Elisha seemed to be continually out and among all types of people, whereas God quite noticeably reserved Elijah for prophecies to and confrontations with the high and the mighty, the kings, queens and priests of Israel. The role of Elisha's wonders and workings is so great that for its complete a thoroughly researched and lengthy work is necessary. He above all others was the prophet who performed miracles to the extent he may merit the title of the "Miracle Man." With widows, children, the poor and oppressed he was always working, and his reputation grew apace. As we associate Elijah with the spectacular and the dramatic, we link Elisha with the quieter side of God's workings, but is this not in many ways the very essence of Christianity? Christ spoke to the disciples not of great cataclysmic events, but rather of the quieter, less noticed matters which are the part and parcel of everyone's everyday life. Yet He above all others knew the true worth of the oft overlooked for He assured His disciples that:

> "...whosoever shall give to drink unto one of these little ones a cup of cold water ... shall in no wise lose his reward."

So, it was with the prophet Elisha, a life, a very long life of endless deeds of demonstrated benevolence of miracles. Often did ordinary persons benefit from his words of blessing, the ill from some "small" miracle of healing or the destitute receive sustenance from his performance as a faithful prophet of God. More than is imagined or for which he is credited Elisha is one of the major figures of the Old Testament. Just a brief analysis will reveal that almost the entire first half of the Book of II Kings is devoted to Elisha.

Neither literally, though, nor in historical reputation did Elisha dwell in secret or perform his deeds in the shadows. As the years followed Elisha's reputation grew great among the high and mighty, just as at an apparent early stage it was well established among the more common people. For one man, not even an Israelite and in reality, a high leader of a foreign enemy power, it proved very fortuitous indeed that the prophet's reputation was widespread even to the Kingdom's most humble servants. The man's name was Naaman, and he was a Syrian, but not just any Syrian. He was a military leader of great renown, the "captain of the host of the King of Syria" and

"...a great man with his master." Naaman was a "great" man, a great warrior of valor, a commander of a powerful army of a mighty nation held in high esteem by his King. He was also a leper. This meant he was afflicted with a torturous disease, relentlessly progressive and distorting of face and body and one which set the afflicted apart from all others in society. Even today the term "leper" though rarely employed to describe a person who actually suffers the disease is a codeword for an outcast, social, moral or physical, and is descriptive of a person of whom very few want any contact. In Biblical days and among the Jews the leper was physically set apart, he was declared "unclean" by the priests and his life become that of a beggar, depending upon the sympathies of others. Yet Naaman was not a Jew, but a Syrian, who had a very active role in society. The Jews, very clean, orderly and meticulous by nature and by law would have isolated a man such as Naaman. The Syrians, Gentiles that they were, did not.

So, what was leprosy and why was it such a terror. The leprosy of the Bible apparently was not the leprosy which remains extant in the modern world. The ancient disease, so common and frequently discussed in the Bible, was not really a skin disease, but rather a disorder of the nervous system. Not necessarily a fatal disease, leprosy alone rarely killed anyone. Neither did it ever go away, and the torment of its sufferers grew more debilitating and ceased only in death. All portions of the body would suffer and especially the face, neck, arms, hands and legs. Eruptions of the skin were frequent, and the leper would suffer increasing distortion of limbs and disfigurement until the hands, for example, would become so gnarled that they more resembled animal claws than human appendages. Leprosy, though, was not painful by any measure. Since it was a nerve disease the complex nervous system of the body would commence a slow of orgy of self-destruction and the loss of the sensation of pain would lead to many hideous and repulsive results. The face itself would distort and often the victim's nose would begin to collapse. The limbs of the body would contort and leave the victim in a repulsive, repugnant shape. The loss of the sensation of pain led the sufferer to absorb more and more damage unknowingly, for even a cup of boiling water thrown on his poor body would not be noticed. Leprosy was a lifelong, slowly developing malady, but its worst characteristic was that it was incurable. It afflicted the humble and the great, even generals such as Naaman. It would be the obstinance, the pride and the vanity of this Syrian warrior, though, that would provide a beautiful and humbling lesson in God's almost infinite patience, not only to Naaman, but also instructive to all still today.

Naaman was a great man with a great household, and likely a great number of servants, among which was one described only as a "little maid," an Israelite, a young Jewish girl who had been kidnapped and enslaved by the victorious Syrian army. She was the servant to Naaman's wife and evidently possessed of a sympathetic heart for she informed her mistress that there was in Samaria a prophet who could cure Naaman of his leprosy. How easily could the great lady scoff at such religious mumbo-jumbo from a young girl, an adherent to the backward superstitions of the Jews, yet she did not. Instead word of this made its path all the way to the throne of the King of Syria himself, who was in no manner dismissive of this knowledge. Actually, the King's response was overwhelmingly favorable and positive, and he authorized Naaman to travel to Israel with a letter of authorization from the King of Syria as well as ten talents of silver and six thousand pieces of gold as a tribute for the "King" to heal Naaman of leprosy. Yes, the King. The mighty, mental machinations of the political class are always a wonder to behold and doubtless a continual trial of God's patience. The Syrian king knew of a cure to be found in Israel, and automatically presumed that its presumptive performer was another king. The arrogance and natural self-importance of the ruling classes have marched through all history with the human race. We see them in the modern guise, not necessarily in royalty, but in elected officials, bureaucrats and assorted experts who have an innate sense of superiority. They all try the patience of others, and how must the patience of God be continually strained by them.

The offer to Israel's King was a disaster, for he suspected an insult from the Syrian monarch. He was fully cognizant that he could not cure leprosy. His anger was kindled and in that ancient gesture of rage he "rent his clothes" and accused the Syrian king of trying to instigate a war. This is some form of diplomatic maneuver in which the King of Israel shall be the loser. Fortunately, news of this fiasco came within the ken of the one man in Israel who could provide a satisfactory solution, the prophet Elisha. Although it is not mentioned Elisha likely was aghast that one king would offer to another a small fortune for the performance of a spiritual deed. In its many forms and visages, it certainly was not an uncommon act in the scriptures, and the patience of God must remain sorely tried with those who seek to purchase and make merchandise of spiritual gifts and matters. Yet Elisha still summoned Naaman to his house.

It is highly unlikely that the captain of the Syrian host was accustomed to being called to the humble home of a foreign holy man, this Israelite prophet who practiced a strange religion and moral code few others could grasp. Yet he went and "...stood at the door of the house of Elisha," awaiting its opening and his first vision and acquaintance with the prophet. Naaman's vanity, though, was just as advanced a disease as his leprosy, and no prophet appeared. A man of that stature summons, and the summoned come. He speaks and his servants and soldiers quickly obey, but here he is not given the expected courtesy of appearance of the man he has traveled hundreds of miles to see and is "wroth".

Naaman's pride has been wounded severely and his temper is rising. Further, he is a man with the acumen and the means to do something violent with that temper. Elisha, though, has not ignored

Naaman or even brushed the Syrian aside. Rather, Elisha sent a messenger to Naaman with the instructions for his healing, for the redemption of his weary body from the unending ravages of leprosy. Yet, the message seems to Naaman as horrible as the disease.

"Go and wash in Jordan seven times, and thy flesh shall come again to thee, and thou shalt be clean."

Naaman, stunned and angry, stalked off in a rage that anyone, least of all an Israelite prophet would so condition the rescue of his health on something as grotesque as immersing seven times in the fabled Jordan River. The Jordan is the sight of many famous events in Bible history, but beautiful and pristine it is not. It is in most places a sluggish, meandering, silt-filled, brown stream of unappealing liquid. Naaman, his pride and vanity injured was not expecting such as this, for even he, the leper, had a differing vision of how he would be healed. He had expected the humbled Elisha to come to greet him, stand and call upon the name of his God, striking Naaman with his rod and the leprosy vanish. In stark human terms he was the patient coming to the physician and telling him how he should be cured. Elisha, though, was a man who Naaman had yet to meet, so Naaman's impatience was kindled and his vanity enraged by the instructions of Elisha's God. He desired to set the terms and conditions of his own salvation, a human frailty that to this day and forever in this world plagues mankind. He willingly and enthusiastically accepted the gift of God so long as it accorded with Naaman's own rather elevated concepts of pride and dignity.

But seven immersions in the filthy Jordan River? He had made the long journey to the arid land of Israel with joyous anticipation of healing in a dramatic scene with a holy man and in which Naaman himself would be the leading man. Seven times in the filth and sludge of the Jordan River? Why seven and why the Jordan? Naaman even makes a counteroffer that if he must do this why not the more beautifully sparkling pure streams of Abana and Paharpur in his own country. No response comes and Naaman, hurt, disappointed, crushed "...turned and walked away in a rage." His regression to Syria, though, is instantly halted by his own servants who approached him with a question as pertinent now as it was then:

> "(I)f the prophet had bid thee do some great thing, wouldst thou not have done it? how much rather then, when he saith to thee, Wash and be clean?"

With almost surgical precision his humble servants excavated deep spiritual truths and extracted a nugget of pure platinum, expressed so beautifully in their own rhetorical question to their master. The Lord of Hosts, the Creator, the God of Heaven and Earth does not expect our lives to go from one mountain peak of glory and achievement to another. Our lives are not to be panoramas of successive scenes of almost Shakespearean drama where we are glorified by doing "great deeds." If we seek that from religion, we will be disappointed and we will suffer failure, just as this great Syrian warrior is on the brink of doing.

Unlike many powerful and successful men who at some juncture in their rise cease listening to anything but flattery, the good sense and cooler reason of Naaman prevailed. After all the delay, the arguing, the tantrums and an attitude which would have exhausted the patience of any man or woman still the longsuffering God remained and so:

> "Then went Naaman down, and dipped himself seven times in Jordan, according to the saying of the man of God: and his flesh came again like unto the flesh of a little child, and he was clean."

Undoubtedly Naaman dreaded immersing himself in the filthy waters seven times over, fully and reasonably expecting to emerge as filthy as the river. Instead, he has what people, especially in the modern age, covet, the healed flesh and beautiful complexion of a child. Do we not hear an early harbinger of words more beautifully spoken centuries later by Christ Himself.

"Whosoever shall not receive the Kingdom of God as a little child shall in no wise enter therein."

Evidently, as God does with all His creation, He was seeking from Naaman many things, and in Naaman's story we discover a splendid showcase for the character of God.

Among those many things which Naaman needed to revise in his character was a pride, a vanity which was literally standing between him and healing. From the beginning to end Naaman was aided not by the "good and the great" but rather by the humble. A "little" (the scripture's exact wording), Israelite slave girl pointed to Naaman's wife the direction in which his salvation lay. The Kings of two famous countries, Israel and Syria, intervene, but their roles are those of hindrance rather than help. One king assumed that if any man possessed the gifts of healing it assuredly had to be another king, while that king saw nothing but trickery and diplomatic treachery. Then, to Naaman's great chagrin and fiery anger it was not the famed prophet who brought Naaman instructions, but instead another servant. Naaman's pride demanded that he be a leading star in a dramatic rendering of his own healing rather than suffer indignities. (How we are compelled to contrast this with the Roman centurion whose faith, centuries later, led him to say to Christ, say the word only, and my servant shall be healed.) In the end, though, Naaman's pride, vanity and dignity fall, at least to manageable levels, as the patience of God is assuaged by the one thing God desired then, now and forever – obedience. To receive the salvation of healing, a free gift, he merely had to obey. The lessons for the present and so obvious that they need hardly be drawn. God's patience is tried, bent and broken with abundance daily by those who reject Him, those who want salvation on theirs, rather than God's terms. It is a free gift, but the last words Christ spoke to His apostles were to go unto all the world "...teach all nations, baptizing them in the name of the Father, and the Son, and the Holy Spirit." This short essay is not proper for any lengthy exposition on Christian apologetics or ethics, yet the story of Elisha and Naaman illustrates so well that salvation is a free gift which we accept with our obedience.

As for Elisha himself he refused Naaman's offer of money and property in exchange for the gift of healing, thereby honoring God and shaming all those who in the Biblical turn of phrase "make merchandise" of religion.

The healing of Naaman is one of many events in Elisha's life, most of which involve his employment of miraculous powers to further the Word of God. As earlier remarked his life's work was not filled with the contention and spectacle as was Elijah's, but Elisha's sojourn on earth was longer. For some fifty-five years he was the leading prophet of the age until passing from life at approximately ninety years of age. He passed from this life, but the miracle man apparently reserved one more thereafter. A funeral procession passed by Elisha's grave and the Israelite mourners were attacked by Moabite raiders. Panicked, the mourners lowered the casket into a nearby tomb, the tomb of Elisha. When the corpse touched the bones of Elisha, it revived and stood up. Even in death Elisha was a life giver. The prophet was also a man who is his well-chronicled life seemed never to have crossed the threshold of God's patience.

Chapter 10

AMOS AND HOSEA – TIMES ARE GETTING HARD

When any review and history of the ancient prophets and God's patience is undertaken eventually a central obstacle must be confronted, and that is the erosion of the reader's interest by the seemingly unending repetition of events. As the years, the decades, the generations and even the centuries roll past we rightfully begin to ask ourselves "Have we not already read about this," and yet the story goes on almost unendingly, often with the only alterations being the names of the participants. Yet therein lies one of the central reasons for the testing of anyone's patience. Most persons get bored with situations that continually repeat themselves, with no progress and with oftentimes the same men and women performing the same roles in identical manners in which they had acted previously. Unfortunately, though, any study of patience, whether human or Divine, is required to include copious amounts of repetition, for it is the repetition of a distasteful act, a rebellious deed, a deplorable manner of conduct wherein the virtue of patience is truly tested.

A parent, save those with hair-trigger tempers, develops a tolerance for occasional misconduct. A child's bad attitude, indolence or even an act of outright disobedience will not (and should not) seal a child's fate with the wrathful doom of the father or mother. Tolerance, though, does not necessarily equate to approval. The years of a child's growth and maturity should reveal a corresponding growth and maturity in the parents, and the manner in which certain situations are handled will be altered, with the parent-child dynamic being modified accordingly. The wise parent, without compromising morality or principles in any manner will grow with the child and the passage of years. Stated in a very plain manner, the parent will not react to an eighteen-year-old young adult in the same fashion as she did when the child was a two-year-old. The difficulty, though, is found in those relationships where the eighteen-year-old continually behaves as a two-year-old toddler. Therein lies the repetition and the parent, often in a literal sense, will scream "Shouldn't you be beyond this behavior?" Therein lay the majority of Israel's testing of God's patience, a patience which was drained, sapped and eventually exhausted. Israel, in age, teaching, blessings and benefits was a mature nation, taken by God in its infancy, provided for, loved and even, at times, pampered. A couple hundred years elapsed, however, and Israel remained a child, insistent on repeating the same deeds over and over. This tested God's patience far beyond human, but not Divine limits, yet even He eventually had His fill of their behavior and rebellion. Yet the God of Creation still willingly offered His people in the ten northern tribes the opportunity of redemption.

Following the death of the great prophet Elisha early in the eighth century B.C. in a moral and religious sense little changed in Israel. It does not follow, however, that all matters remained the same. Israel, growing prosperous in the reign of Ahab decades earlier continued its upward momentum towards the "good life." It had secured and maintained good relations with many, but not all, its neighbors.

Trade and mercantile routes had been secured, and even ancient manufacturing industries had developed, all with the result that more Israelites benefited from the enjoyment of prosperity. Some, enough so that they constituted a social class, were able to partake freely from the delights of luxurious living. None of these matters is the subject of a per se condemnation anywhere in either the Old or New Testaments. All come, though, with plentiful warnings that the dangers of prosperity and particularly, luxury, offer. The same old maladies afflicted Israel, and for these God offered the same remedies, still unheeded, as before. The great prophetic duo of Elijah and Elisha was gone, in their ability and greatness the epitome of admirable spiritual leadership, yet God's quiver was not without arrows. He made the path for other prophets, and the two most noteworthy were Amos and Hosea, apparently contemporaries for a time and surely men who knew or knew of each other.

Amos is first to appear, and, in many ways, he is as much as enigmatic figure as was the great Elijah. Amos emerges as a simple man with a simple, unpretentious name and the spokesman of a simple, unadorned yet overwhelmingly powerful prophecy. Our knowledge of his background is sparing. He came from the village of Tekoa six miles south of another village which would later gain at least a nominal amount of fame, Bethlehem. Thus, he was a southerner, a native of Judah, but a man who was commissioned primarily to speak to the northern neighbors in Israel. In his own words he introduced himself as a "...herdsman and a gatherer of sycamore fruit." Amos possessed no pedigree as a prophet or a prophet's son and openly admitted he was merely a shepherd. The student and observer are compelled to remark about God's penchant for choosing and favoring shepherds for important work.

Here we must turn to Amos's prophetic commission and the repetition of the message due to the people's repetition of behavior. A central theme of Amos's teachings and prophecy was the moral, social and political corruption which Israel's prosperity had engendered. Noted earlier in Chapter Four had been the rise of social classes and castes, opprobrious to God. As overemployed and trite as the statement may be truly were "...the rich getting richer and the poor, poorer." It was not a simple divergence of the path of economic indicators but rather the oppression which many of the new rich utilized to squeeze the less wealthy. Taxes had increased, foreclosures on land, and homes had become commonplace, all in the midst of unprecedented prosperity. Under the leadership of King Jeroboam II Israel had expanded its borders, reclaimed its ancient territories east of the Jordan River and extended its borders northward even to parts of Phoenicia.

What a wonderful time it was to be a rich Israelite, and so Amos noticed and duly and forthrightly recorded. In the beautifully descriptive language of the scriptures he saw many who could now "...lie upon beds of ivory, and stretch themselves upon their couches." Like scenes from a twentieth century ancient Hollywood spectacular they reclined on their couches, lapping the finest wines from bowls and soothed and comforted themselves with the latest music. For a certain class, indeed life was good. The condemnations of the Israelites were harsh, as their sins and transgressions were enormous. Yet have we, and especially the ancient Israelites, not heard different versions of these words from different prophets many times before? A resounding "Yes" must be the response, but this time mere chastisement and moral condemnation do not conclude the matter. The days of feasts will be turned to mourning and the land would be blighted with famine:

> "...I will send a famine in the land, not a famine of bread, nor a thirst for water, but of hearing the words of the Lord."

Amos continued at length with vivid prophecies, but hardly understood by many, ignored by most and kept by God. Surely, though, one extraordinary stark warning must have taken aback all who heard it, as Amos explained the Israelites' futility in escaping death:

> "Though they dig into hell, thence shall mine hand
> take them; though they climb up to heaven, thence
> will I bring them down."

As if to hammer the prophecy into the hearts of its hearers Amos added that Israel "...shall fall and never rise up again." Apocalyptic words for certain, but what did they mean? Was Amos prophesying in fact, the apocalypse, the end of all things for Israel. To aid in their understanding Amos briefly recounted to the Israelites not their destruction, but a history of continuous deliverance and salvation by their God. He asks them "Have not I brought up Israel out of the land of Egypt?" Yet he turns and slams his hearers that now God is ready to destroy this kingdom from the face of the earth. These are the emotions and words of a God of patience, patience that has seemed endless, enduring some three centuries of Israel's perfidy, a patience finally exhausted.

Amos takes his rightful place in the front rank of Hebrew prophets who were unafraid to employ words as spears and arrows to pierce to the very marrow of the listener's bones or to wield them as maces and clubs to stun the hearers. Nothing aroused the prophet and caused his harsh words to reverberate and echo than the injustice which he saw had become almost endemic in Israelite society. With no sense of delicacy and what in modern parlance is denominated "political correctness" the prophet addressed the "cattle" of Bashan, which "oppress the poor" and "crush the needy". Especially and pointedly did he refer to certain rich, indolent, leisure addicted women as "fat cows" whose sins were about to catch up with them.

On no subject, however, was this prophet of God more scathingly and bitterly eloquent than on the subject of the artificial, hypocritical religion and their offerings which they continued to present to the one true God. Israel, even in its blackest depths, had not fully abandoned an acknowledgment and worship of God, but He had been reduced in stature to become just one of many gods and deities which they worshipped, just like the pagan Gentiles who surrounded them. Amos again demonstrated that nothing incenses God more than false displays of religious devotion and piety. Yes, the Israelites still kept many of the forms of the Law, the pilgrimages, the sacrifices and the feast days, but they were an abomination to Him:

> "I hate, I despise your feast days, and I will not smell in your assemblies. Though you offer me burnt offerings and your meat offerings, I will not accept them: neither will I regard the peace offerings of your fat beasts."

God added that He was tired of their singing songs to Him and making any kind of sacrifice. The Israelites had committed the great profanation of placing the pagan gods Moloch and Chiun in the tabernacle and their giving homage to them. How similar in tone and substance is this to these words later spoken by Christ:

> "This people draweth nigh unto me with their mouth, and honoreth me with their lips; but their heart is far from me."

With full confidence and the inspiration of God Himself Amos could effectively assert that nothing is more revolting, more nauseating and repulsive to God than false, or "phony" religion, a religion of which the Israelites maintained great and mountainous heaps. Starkly God said through his prophet "Do not even go through the motions of worship to Me" for I know its true lack of sincerity and value. These are the thoughts and the speech of a God of almost infinite patience who is about to reveal the terrible consequences of actually exhausting that patience. This time the prophet's words did not fall on deaf ears, like in the days of Isaiah in Judah. Amos spoke so sharply, so vigorously and so lividly it was inevitable that his prophecy would be met with some reaction, and it was.

We must remember that in no sense was Amos a seasoned veteran of prophecy, apparently lacking that type of training or schooling. In later and still extant terms Amos was in no sense a member of the clergy, but rather a humble shepherd and keeper of fruit trees. Israel, though, by this point in its history had developed a quite detailed religious structure of priests and prophets, some of God but far more of the imported Gentile variety. As does the clergy of almost all ages and religions this clergy rigidly guarded its station and privileges and deeply resented the intrusion of an uncredentialed interloper upon the sacred grounds of their profession, a resentment and hatred which later attain its zenith in the fear and hatred of the Jewish religious establishment for Jesus Christ. Among this ilk was a priest of Bethel, a prominent town eleven miles north of Jerusalem. His name was Amaziah, and he believed that Amos had snared himself in a trap which would allow for his easy destruction. Amaziah obtained an audience with Israel's King Jeroboam II, and he gave him the horrendous news that Israel would be taken captive and Jeroboam himself murdered. With the undoubted royal backing of Jeroboam, Amaziah informed Amos that he was ordered to return to his native land of Judah and do his prophesying there. Amaziah exercised the contempt the trained professional has for the uneducated and untrained amateur and haughtily told Amos to prophesy and sport himself with his own kind. In other words, Amos you lack the training, the background and the approval of the elites which gives you a prophet his authority. Amos did not take Amaziah's bait, and he even readily admitted that he was no prophet but rather a humble shepherd and herdsman. He carried with him, however, one thing which neither Amaziah nor his colleagues could claim, and that was the authority and commission of God. In a scene which would be repeated eight centuries later before the Jewish Sanhedrin, the apostles Peter and John were scorned as "ignorant and unlearned men," yet that was not sufficient obstacle to deter them from teaching and preaching the things they had heard and seen. So, Amos returned to the land of Judah after an Israelite sojourn of heaping coals of fire upon its inhabitants and warning them of the horrors that awaited them in the impending collapse, captivity and enslavement of the entire nation.

Stunningly, strikingly the Divine patience of God is not yet exhausted, for in the thundering words of doom which Amos spoke to Israel the patience of God was revealed again: For thus saith the Lord of Israel, seek ye me, and ye shall live."

God had one messenger remaining, a man as overlooked as Amos, but just as important and the final bearer of light before the darkness permanently engulfed this northern kingdom of Israel. His name was Hosea (looking and sounding Spanish nevertheless it was Hebrew), and to Hosea was given the most unusual mission of any prophet. It has often been remarked that people would rather see a story than hear one any day, and this has been remarked in many manners throughout the ages. Most beautifully was it expressed in a non-scriptural setting, assumedly by St. Francis of Assisi who in the Middle Ages expressed the beautiful thought that we should "...(P) reach the gospel always; use words only when necessary." God has often employed many words, and so He did with Hosea; however, this prophet was given the task of illustrating with his own life the expanse and depths of God's love.

After several centuries of Israel's Biblical "...whoring after false gods," God Himself must have felt violated. To starkly and boldly illustrate such He opens the Book of Hosea with an astounding directive to the prophet:

> "...(T)ake unto thee a wife of whoredoms and children of whoredoms: for the land hath committed great whoredom, departing from the Lord."

Remarkably, the God of Israel, the progenitor of The Ten Commandments just instructed His holy prophet to marry a prostitute. In human everyday speech God seems to imply His rationale to Hosea. Effectively, wed yourself to a prostitute, a low person in any society in any age, and you will see how I, your God, has felt for many centuries. Effectively, He makes the point that being Israel's God is very much akin to being married to a prostitute, a person who is unfaithful by habit and by design. The obedient Hosea finds a prostitute-bride with a name that is startling to twenty-first century English speakers but nonetheless her name Gomer. Rather than having a wife of high character and reputation, a desire on any decent man, Hosea is now known to the world as the husband of a harlot. Through Hosea, God declares essentially now you should see and sense how I, your God, feels. Spiritually, the Lord expounds, I am married to the harlot of Israel, a nation and people who refuse to be faithful.

Gomer bears Hosea three children, but only the first, Jezreel, having Hosea as a father with the second and third, Jehu and Zechariah having unknown fathers. Unknown to us, but likely known by their contemporaries in this small, ancient society, thereby making Hosea bear the humiliation of being a cuckolded husband. There, God seems to be saying, you now know how I feel.

The burdens God placed on His prophet Hosea were enormous, burdens that no man would want to go near, yet Hosea as a man proved his great worth and merit by his conduct in the throes of humiliating circumstances. Not only did he so, but the great prophet employed this abysmal situation as an allegorical teaching instrument to forthrightly illustrate to the Israelites how God felt about their behavior. Yet as abhorrent and prevalent as was the actual practice of adultery among the Israelites even more grotesque was the "spiritual" adultery and outright ingratitude demonstrated by most of the people. As if it were not enough that the Israelites gave no thanks to God for their prosperity, no gratitude for the safe and pleasant lives they were enjoying they actually attributed their bounty and good fortune to another god – Baal. Yes, that Baal and all his associate pagan gods of the Canaanites. To them did the heart of Israel really belong, and to God they were Israel's "lovers" lovers to whom Israel sacrificed, billowed and cooed. Sweetness and light while God emphatically states that:

> "She did not know that I gave her corn, and wine,
> and oil and multiplied her silver and gold, which
> they prepared for Baal."

Israel was a spouse, a pampered, self-expectant hedonist who lavishly enjoyed her blessings and attention, and in response gave her attention and gratitude to other men, much as Gomer had done with Hosea. Likely only the man or woman who has been the victim of adultery can even commence to contemplate the pain and emotional tidal wave which consumes the spouse who has been so victimized. God so understood those emotions, and so now did His prophet Hosea.

As for the suffering Hosea let us now examine his plight and his options of behavior. Married, publicly and most certainly privately disgraced and humiliated to this wife's rejection is added the knowledge of her dalliances with other men. Under the Law Hosea's rights were to divorce her, and in the overwhelmingly majority of cases this is likely the outcome for a multiple adulterer. God established laws, and both Testaments are evidence that He expected and till expects the fulfillment of His commandments. Yet God goes beyond His law at times and exercises two qualities of which He has in magnificent abundance, grace and mercy, and often He expects it from His disciples. Hosea's shame is ongoing, for she was living with her latest paramour. Go to your adulterous wife, said God to Hosea, have mercy and buy her back from the man with whom she is living. The redemption price for Gomer was fifteen shekels, and to Hosea, a wronged man, and a true victim, she returned. The image, the allegory and the metaphor of God's redeeming the sinner from the death of sin immediately touches as the story of Gomer's redemption being symbolic of God's ultimate redemption of humanity by the sacrifice of Jesus Christ.

We will now indulge in a bit of our own repetition. So, the God of the Old Testament was wrathful, hard to please and a flame throwing tyrant always ready to crush and destroy even His own disciples. To many, those always heedful of the popular consensus, He is a truly fearful being, almost impossible to approach, a distinctly frightful entity always ready to crush the sinner for the slightest error, misstep or miscalculation. He is said to remember not only every sin, but every slight and perceived insult and seemingly enjoys the destruction of His own creation. How little do image and reality here correspond, and in the vernacular but in the obvious, nothing could be further from the truth. At this juncture it is unfathomable to us but a pleading God, a Father who is almost begging to offer forgiveness to His children with such enticements as these:

> "Behold, I will allure her, and bring her into the wilderness, and speak comfortably unto her. And I will give her vineyards from thence, and the valley of Achar for a door of hope: and she shall sing there, as in the day when she came up out of the land of Egypt."

A view of God which sees a Deity willing and eager to punish is certainly not found in the New Testament, wherein God appeared in human form as the lowly Jesus of Nazareth, the Prince of Peace. It is the same God read about in the turning leaves of the Old Testament, a God whose love and patience seem to have no terminal point, who goes far beyond the self-imposed boundaries of humans and rushes to offer forgiveness. Yes, His patience seemingly is endless, yet "seemingly" and "certainly" are not the same words.

The ancient would was a brutal place, not merely rough, tough and primitive, but it was almost unfailingly, piteously and sadistically brutal. Depending upon a person's historical proclivities we in the West trace out Western Civilization to the ancient Greeks and Romans, later tempered and molded by the changes wrought by the coming and leavening influences of the Hebrew Biblical teachings and the advent of Christianity. The ancient Greek civilization, especially that borne and nurtured in the great city – state of Athens remains, and in many instances deservedly so, a touchstone and beacon for guidance. their development of arts and sciences and the first staffing of participatory government remain inspirational. The rise, power, authority and longevity of Rome remains so influential in the West, especially among those lands with Latin origins. Its organizational methods, legal system and especially in its earlier republican form representative government remain exemplary. The old nations, governments and most of their structures and edifices are long gone, yet a wise person still sees Greece and Rome as the two standards of civilization in early history. Yet even they routinely and often with an almost diabolical glee, seemed almost to make hideous brutality a portion of everyday life. The internecine warfare of the Greeks, yes, the noble intellectual Greeks, had its theater of operations continuously floating upon a sea of blood. The Romans, so practical and so organized, conducted official operations with an almost bureaucratic efficiency, its victorious armies either enslaving their forces or butchering them by the tens of thousands, not necessarily as the practice of sadism but rather to be more efficient and thorough in their battlefield triumphs. Even their criminal punishments were conducted with a sort of bizarre, even Satanic, cruelty, reaching their pinnacle in crucifixion, a subject upon which no reader off this work needs further instruction. These were the "civilizations" of the ancient world for which rightly we both admire and deplore.

It was not all the glory of Greece and grandeur of Rome, however. to them we add an endless parade of names, Phoenicia, Philistia, Canaan, Syria, Egypt, Moab, Persia, Babylon and on it goes, and except for the expert academic specialist all begin to blend one into another. All, that is, but one – Assyria, the land of the real terrors and tyrants of the ancient world. It is to these people that God would finally consign His own chosen people. A nation that had freed from Egyptian enslavement would now be grist for the mill of a nation far stricter and gruesome in its behavior than were the Egyptian's. An empire that began on with the small city-state of Ashur, sited on the western banks of the Tigris River in what is now northern Iraq, it gradually expanded and is frequently mentioned in Old Testament scriptures and was often a major player in the political and military struggles in the Middle East. Its expansion, with certain setbacks, continued into the 700's B.C., wherein the Old Testament itself continuously alludes to its threat to both Israel and Judah. It had been a terrible almost unspeakable menace on the northern borders of Israel for three centuries. Through alliances, timely incompetent Assyrian leadership and a protective Divine Hand Israel retained an assumed security behind its borders.

Finally, though, in a series of actions which culminated in the calamity of 722 B.C., God removed the hand of protection and the Assyrians arrived as Amos had prophesized to "...take you away with hooks and your posterity with fishhooks," a grim reference to the

Assyrian custom of chaining together its captives with hooks piercing through their lips. Yet this awaited only the captives strong enough to survive battle and siege. Typically, the Assyrians would besiege a city, in Israel's case the capital of Samaria, and stage a continual "show" to impress its cornered enemies with the fates that awaited them. In full view of the besieged city the Assyrian soldiers would torture their enemies, often flaying them and peeling the skin from their bodies. Captives would be quartered and butchered like livestock, but only after having their noses and ears chopped off and their eyes blinded. In a fate common to women in all wars the captive women would be stripped naked by the Assyrians, and their humiliation advanced by mass rape.

Those that survived faced the terrors of slavery, a catastrophic infliction anywhere by anyone but particularly onerous by Assyrian standards. Assyrian slavery had a purpose, and it seems that its primary purpose was to build what we now call the "infrastructure" of empire, the various buildings, palaces and temples that required brutally hard work by massive quantities of slaves whose lives were dispensable. The Israelites suffered all this and more as they were crushed under the tyrannical power of ancient history's foremost survivors. Some did survive, though, and gradually intermarried and assimilated into pagan Assyrian culture and society, losing all separate identity as Israelites and Jews. In an almost directly reverse fashion the same result, though, without most of the terror, awaited those scatterings of Jews who survived and remained behind in Israel. The Assyrians were great colonizers, and by forced immigration they settled other ethnicities into their newly acquired territory of Israel. They, too, intermarried with the Israelites and became known as the Samaritans, a people of great prominence in the New Testament story.

So in the end the northern nation of Israel faded into oblivion and those ten tribes who with pride could trace their inception to the sons of Jacob, were gone. The names and tribes of Reuben, Simeon, Dan, Gad, Asher, Naphtali, Zebulon, Manasseh, Issachar and Ephraim were historically obliterated. As a separate nation God had expended upon them three centuries of care, concern, love, protection, understanding and patience. Some of the great names in not only Bible, but all history, notably Elijah and Elisha, devoted their lives and energies to them. Yet the ignored for three hundred years the love and patience of God, until time finally ran out. The Promise, though, lived in the southern nation of Judah, and to it we now focus our attention.

Chapter 11

JEREMIAH – BLOWING IN THE WIND

A common trait and a common bond of almost all humanity in all ages, places and circumstances is the desire to enjoy the lives they have been given. Although it may seem otherwise, it truly is the rare person who is indifferent to happiness and pleasures, and in fact such a person in the extreme has often been more feared than pitied. Living, though, makes us aware that many persons have little or no happiness in their lives, whether by accident, ill health or other emotional and physical circumstances. Some, we must concede, we wish to see at some level of unhappiness, those being the cruel, the malignant and the criminal. From time immemorial prisons have been constructed, and for the most heinous of crimes society consigns to the worst of them the worst offenders, the rapists and the murderers. Whether admitted or not the typical individual does not desire that such persons "have a good day," and they wish for them to suffer misery and unhappiness, perhaps even for the remainder of their lives.

Yet all the preceding are to a greater or lesser extent personal choices. Let us consider a person who through no natural inclination of his own is specifically chosen to pursue a career and a life which in the main will deliver to him discomfort, unhappiness and misery. Not just a "life" either but an especially long life where he witnesses so much and is afflicted with so much darkness of the soul that he earns a title by which he has been known throughout history, that of the "Weeping Prophet"? Further he views so much and is so persecuted that later in life he is moved to write a book known simply as "Lamentations." He had much to lament, and though he did not want the role a young Jeremiah was chosen by God Himself to display a tenacity, a strength of character and physical and moral discipline that in later historic company with the apostles few have ever known.

Jeremiah was from the southern kingdom of Judah and made his first appearance in this world in approximately 640 B.C., at the lowest point in Judah's history shortly after the death of its long ruling king, Manasseh, whose thirty-five year reign had witnessed the national humiliation of Judah's becoming a compliant vassal state to the mighty Assyrian empire. Not content with political abasement Manasseh had reintroduced Canaanite paganism, and temples to such gods as Baal and Moloch proliferated. Manasseh, whose own father had been the great and good King Hezekiah, set a new low for apostate immorality when he gave his own sons as sacrificial burnt offerings to the pagan deities. A legendary tradition has it that Manasseh placed in the great temple at Jerusalem an idol with four faces, one in each direction, so its gaze could not be missed by any Temple entrant.

Into this moral morass to which King Manasseh had enthusiastically led the people of Judah was borne Jeremiah to whom God first spoke in 627 B.C., when Jeremiah was but an adolescent, perhaps thirteen years old. He spoke tremendously powerful words to Jeremiah in phrases the impact of which revealed God's thinking to the youth and on other matters to us now:

"Before I formed thee... I knew thee; and before
though camest out of the womb I sanctified thee,
and I ordained thee a prophet unto the nations."

Powerful, mighty, tremendous, cataclysmic speech from God
Himself, and it elicited from the young adolescent Jeremiah a response easily identifiable to all of us, in that "...I cannot speak, for I
am a child." Easily the Lord could have responded to Jeremiah with
such words as "Son, I have heard such before," and certainly He had.
Centuries prior at the Burning Bush Moses emptied his mind and
possibly even his soul of reasons and excuses or why he was not the
man to confront Pharaoh and free the Israelites. As God had patience with Moses so likewise did He with Jeremiah. Yet God was
adamant that Jeremiah was the chosen vessel for a task as difficult
as was laid on Moses's shoulders. Among other demonstrations of
God's character is that He is never reluctant to employ the young for
the most important, substantive roles. Thoughts go to such youths
as the seventeen-year-old Joseph, the young David conquering the
giant Goliath, Daniel and his companions standing firm in the face
of Nebuchadnezzar and the young, beautiful girl Esther confronting
her husband, the all-powerful King Xerxes of Persia. To this illustri-
ous list was added the name of the young prophet Jeremiah.

In the Bible and for all eternity the wisdom of God is subject to
no limitations. Jeremiah assuredly was to have a long, harsh, punish-
ing life as a prophet, but in his youth, he would have the benefit of
working with another young man, a man who for a generation and
throughout a full generation held the reins of power in Judah. His
name was Josiah, and his story is as meaningful, important and interesting as that of Jeremiah's, and the absence of its brief retelling
would weaken any biography of Jeremiah. At the tender age of eight,
this son of the evil King Manasseh became the King of Judah, but his
royal administration and influence did not really commence until
he reached age sixteen. Unlike a long stream of predecessors Josiah

was different "and he did right in the sight of the Lord and walked in the ways of David his father, and declined neither to the right hand, nor to the left." Judah now possessed a young king who reigned in a kingdom in which a young prophet such as Jeremiah would be honored. From the Biblical times rulers have almost universally sought to be known as "reformers." A magical euphemism which supposedly imbues its holder with the ability, the tenacity and the courage to reshape or "re-form" society. Be they king, president, governor or emperor few actually reform anything and so are consigned in an oblivion of forgotten history. Josiah, though, was not just a reformer, for he sought to return or restore Judah to its day of obedience to God. In the forefront of Josiah's restoration campaign was a purge of all heathen temples and worship practices, so that:

> "(I)n the twelfth year he began to purge Judah and
> Jerusalem from the high places, and the groves, and
> the carved images and the molten images."

The pagan idols were toppled, broken into pieces, crushed and even pulverized, and is a starkly symbolic act the dust of the destroyed idols "...was strewn upon the graves of them that had sacrificed unto them." To demonstrate the disgust and even rage of God at the "priests" who had turned Judah to paganism the King burnt their remaining bones upon the altars. In an action that renders the God of Heaven and Earth and the Creator of the Universe as shockingly beyond the pale of modern political correctness he even went so far as to openly attack and eradicate Judah's homosexual community.

Josiah, though, was not just an engine of destruction, however needed that destruction might have been, but he was also highly attuned to constructive work that needed to be done, namely and most prominently the repair and refurbishing of the great Temple, which had been allowed to deteriorate through the decades, an apt metaphor for Judah's spiritual decline and disrepair.

The restoration of the Temple was a massive undertaking with carpenters, masons and stonecutters all employed enmasse. One day the high priest Hilkiah reported that in the reconstruction efforts a book of the law had been found, one of the original Five Books of Moses, the Torah, the Genesis, Exodus, Leviticus, Numbers and Deuteronomy which begin every Bible. Astonishingly Judah had sunk to such a low ebb that no written record of its past, no evidence of the Ten Commandments or any of the law which God had revealed on Sinai to Moses apparently even existed. Upon hearing the reading of the Law King Josiah was so distressed that he tore his clothes (how frequent an Old Testament emotional response) and gloomily foretold that Judah was doomed because of its traditional historic and pervasive disregard of God. Genuine though the King's reaction may have been he was premature, because God's patience still held and extended far beyond the point Josiah thought even possible. Judah yet possessed more life than Josiah, for the good King's days were numbered. He perished in battle against the Egyptians at Megiddo, and at the relatively youthful age of thirty-nine this good man and marvelous king ended his earthly walk. While not the most famous of the monarchs he was perhaps the greatest, for the scriptures provide the glorious benediction that there was:

> "...(N)o king before him, that turned to the Lord with all his heart, and with all his soul, and with all his might, according to all the law of Moses; neither after him arose there any like him."

Truly it was enormously beneficial to the adolescent prophet Jeremiah to effectively come of age during the reign of King Josiah, and it is hard, perhaps even impossible, not to see the directing hand and Spirit of God on providing a period of time and a King such as Josiah who would serve as a buffer from the hatred and persecution which was mounting and which burst forth in a deluge, against

Jeremiah as he grew older and matured. For the ensuing decades Jeremiah could count on one friend and only one, God.

The prophet discovered what multitudes of men and women, especially those who are righteous, learn to their chagrin, and that is the realization that those presumed to be the most loving and supportive, those bound by the ties of blood and lineage often are not, and in reality are either ravening wolves or wolves in sheep's clothing. God Himself, sadly and reluctantly no doubt, informed Jeremiah that he should never expect any help from his own heritage and family for "they ... will deal treacherously with you." Not only treacherously but even worse for his own family will "speak fair words unto thee" while at the same moment be organizing a multitude of opposition against him. After the death of Josiah, the flood of apostasy was not held back for long, and his death signaled the beginning of a kingly succession of four men, sons and grandsons of Josiah, all with the remarkably Old Testament nomenclature of Jehoahaz, Jehoiakim, Jehoiachin and Zedekiah. It is with the second king, Jehoiakim with whom Jeremiah's prophetic path first crossed, and to his reign we look initially. Immediately upon Josiah's death his youngest son, Jehoahaz, a popular figure, was selected by the people to be their ruler, yet his reign lasted a brief three months. The real political power in Judah, though, now was in the hands of Egypt's pharaoh (how history repeats itself) and he preferred the King to be Jehoiakim, the elder brother of Jehoahaz. Jehoiakim's twelve years as king may serve as a template for all Israel's and Judah's apostate kings, for the story of his tenure is so familiar. As both a king and a man Jehoiakim was a repulsive degenerate who "...did what was evil in the sight of the Lord, according to all that his father had done." Jehoiakim's life provides an inventory of political, moral and financial oppression and violence and an abundance of the common crimes of murder, theft, rape and incest. Jehoiakim was in the beginning a fawning vassal of Egypt, but the vassalage would not be of an enduring them.

God offered to Jeremiah a prophetic vision of a boiling pot tilted from the north to the south, an impending peril and danger to anyone or anything that lay under its scalding contents. The danger from the north was the rising power of Babylon, which was well equipped to be God's instrument in visiting destruction upon Judah in the south just as Judah's brother kingdom, Israel, had been destroyed by the Assyrians. Beyond the pale human comprehension, the wide boundaries of God's patience still held in check with His wrath. He related to Jeremiah that His intention was still to be patient and to build in Judah, but in the meantime, Jeremiah was to speak openly in the temple of Jerusalem issuing these phrases for the ears of King Jehoiakim:

> "If you will not listen to me, to walk in my law which
> I have set before you, and to heed the words of my
> servants the prophets whom I send to you urgently...
> I will make this city a curse for all the nations of the
> earth."

If anyone listened to these words of prophetic condemnation, he certainly was not named Jehoiakim. The king and all in Judah have just been handed a promise of condemnation, and he and his cohorts react in rage. Jeremiah is barred from speaking in the Temple, while another prophet, Uriah, does not escape the King's wrath, as Uriah is murdered at Jehoiakim's direction.

Jeremiah may have eluded death at the hands of Jehoiakim, but he does not escape entirely unscathed. Pashur was the chief officer of the Temple and a priest (how often do priests easily exchange their clerical robes for those of villains!) is incensed at Jeremiah's prophecy, and in addition to the speaking ban to be rigidly enforced he has Jeremiah flogged and then suffer the humiliation of being placed in the stocks for public ridicule. Although poor Jeremiah continues to walk a path of suffering upon his release the prophet foretold the doom of Pashur, that he would confront "terror" on every side, that Jerusalem and the Temple would be plundered and that most certainly Pashur and his family would be enslaved as captives by the Babylonians. Jeremiah was barred from the Temple, yet his voice was in no manner muffled.

The modern age is an age of politics and of vast widespread superficial political knowledge, spread across this small globe by every manner of instantaneous technology. God, though, then and now, has always been and remains keenly attuned to politics and the affairs of men and nations but for vastly different reasons than those of the human race. The political and military structure of the ancient world was shifting radically and, in the days, years and centuries would produce changes of cataclysmic dimensions. In the north and west the small rocky land of the Greeks was developing a culture that would conquer the ancient world as much as any army. Even further west a people whose might and power would dwarf that of the Assyrians, the Persians, the Egyptians and all who came before was stirring, and soon Rome would be the center of the world. And what of this tiny sliver of land, this small nation of Judah with their odd beliefs and their weird, eccentric religion? For a certainty only God knew, and he communicated such to His chosen prophet Jeremiah. The oracles of God were then delivered by the prophet to his associate Baruch.

Recorded in the Book of Jeremiah the oracles underscore the parenthetical word in the title of this work, the "Almost" infinity of God's patience. Hundreds of years of disobedience, indolence and rebellion had earlier led to the extinction of Judah's northern brother Kingdom of Israel. Now it was the turn of Judah, a small nation invariably enjoying the protection of God through all manner of situations, but now to suffer as did the Israelites. Babylon, the rising power in the north, a heathen nation with inanimate idols as their deities, was to be God's chosen instrument for Judah's destruction.

Jerusalem would be sacked and plundered, the Temple itself looted of all valuables and desecrated. Vast numbers would meet death at the end of Babylonian weapons, and the remainder, man and woman, high and low, and good and bad would learn firsthand what cruel slavery was. None of these words are pleasing to the ear and some of the King's cohorts, led by the scribe Jehudi, heard them and advised Jeremiah's messenger and Jeremiah himself to go into hiding rather than suffer the King's outrage.

Dutifully the King's servant Jehudi obtained a transcript of the prophecy, unrolled it and began to read it before Jehoiakim and "...the princes which stood beside the king." It was wintertime and the King was warming himself by the hearth in which a fire was giving comfort and warmth to the royal chambers. As Jehudi read the prophecy of disapproval, destruction and doom Jehoiakim calmly took a penknife and cut the words as they were read and tossed them into the fire. He made a thorough task of it, for it was entirely consumed and thus no longer in existence. Calmly, the majestic monarch leans back and without a trace of wrath or even anger, gives orders that Baruch and Jeremiah are to be "taken" the purposes for which are easy to surmise. The two are not to be found, though, because they have been hidden in secret by God.

In a lifetime and a monarchial reign Jehoiakim has blundered, rebelled and plainly went his own way, without any heed of God's wishes. Now, in one gesture he reveals not only his heart and soul but has committed two major mistakes that are quite common yet today. Actually, they are made so frequently and, in all circumstances, and times that it may truly be stated that they are endemic to the human experience. Initially he has blamed the messenger for a bad message. Neither Baruch nor Jeremiah possess the slightest trace of influence on what is to happen. They are unknown to the Babylonian King Nebuchadnezzar. The King's political and military decisions are his own, and although God is about to mold them for His service the

King of Babylon is sending the forces to loot Jerusalem and enslave the population of Judah. It is not Jeremiah who will oust Jehoiakim from his beloved throne, and neither is the prophet to be rightfully blamed for the King's impending demise.

Secondly, Jehoiakim, no doubt from an inner emotional rage, has made the cardinal error, maybe becoming even more common in the complex modern era, of believing that if the evidence of bad news is destroyed then the bad news itself has perished. The King's singular accomplishment has been the conversion of a short tangible document into a handful of ashes, for its underlying truth remains. That verity is that God's patience with Judah, its mostly wretched kings and its weal and disobedient people has attained its concluding chapter. Kill Jeremiah if you like, would say God, but it changes nothing. Just as a couple generations hence would reveal another Divine message to another failed king so is God saying that you, King Jehoiakim, and your entire kingdom has been weighed in the balance and found wanting.

After so protracted a prophecy of its doom it would be easy to declare that the actual destruction of Jerusalem and the exile and captivity of the Jewish people was anti-climactic. It was not, but it did unfold in stages. Judah, a small land, was trapped in a pincer by the movements of two great powers, Egypt and Babylon. The last few years of Jehoiakim's reign saw him and his kingdom reduced to vassalage and servitude. Like a modern Mafioso continually demanding "protection" money Jehoiakim was forced by Babylon to exact and pay a continually escalating tribute to Babylon. Jehoiakim himself, though, possessed pro-Egyptian tendencies and ultimately refused to pay any more tribute extortion to the Babylonians. Nebuchadnezzar's considerable temper and wrath were excited, and his army marched upon Jerusalem to besiege it. Jehoiakim, though, died before the siege's beginning, and he was succeeded by his eighteen-year-old son, Jehoiachin. None of this, though, had any bearing whatsoever upon the plans of the King of Babylon.

The siege of Jerusalem was not a long, continuous ordeal, it being interrupted on at least one occasion. In 597 B.C., though, the determined Babylonians revealed their grim seriousness, besieged the city in earnest and destroyed the city walls. In short order there followed the destruction of the royal palace, almost the entirety of the city's buildings and dwellings and even the great Temple of Solomon, the center of the Jewish faith. Tens of thousands were slaughtered and even more marched in chains to captivity in the strange, alien world of Babylon. Nebuchadnezzar, in an action all too familiar in modern history, now established Judah as a "puppet" kingdom to be ruled by a new "King", who was effectively to be the Babylonian's lapdog. His name was Zedekiah, who replaced Jehoiachin and his brief three-month reign.

Let it not be said that the destruction of Jerusalem and the captivity of the Jews was a calamity that befell only the common people, the poorer classes. The upper strata of society, including and perhaps especially kings and priests suffered dearly. Before destroying the Temple, Nebuchadnezzar's men desecrated it and stole its considerable amounts of gold and silver. More degradation and humiliation awaited and this time it would be meted out to the last royalty in all Israel and Judah, its final King Zedekiah.

Zedekiah was a puppet who broke the strings of the master in Babylon who controlled him. Against the advice of Jeremiah, he made an alliance with Egypt and joined forces to oppose Babylon. An outraged Nebuchadnezzar again threw his mighty army into Judah. The erstwhile ally Egypt quickly abandoned the field, with Zedekiah and his remaining forces to fight the Babylonians, who once again besieged Judah. So terrible was this two-year siege that the "...famine was so severe that there was no food for the people." Jeremiah himself recorded that he witnessed starving mothers cannibalizing their own children.

Finally, the Babylonian soldiers broke through the rebuilt walls in 587 B.C., exacted terrible retribution and pursued the fugitive King Zedekiah and his army. They were overtaken near Jericho, and the King had the honor of being the prized captive. Only the unknowing and the deliberately ignorant believe the Bible to be an endless recounting of beautiful stories and wondrous love, both human and Divine. Both Testaments hold copious amounts of such narratives, but the student knows that Holy Writ is also uncommonly bold in revealing gruesome tales. Zedekiah, the wayward puppet King was bound and forced to witness the systematic execution of all his officials and sons. While the blood still clotted and dripped from the swords of the executioners the King was bound in shackles and his eyes hideously put out. They then transported "...him to Babylon, and put him in prison till the day of his death." One month later the Babylonians added a coda to all this and destroyed, literally burned and razed to the ground what was left of Jerusalem. The great nation ordained by God and led from slavery by Moses was no more. Israel was finished a full 140 years earlier and now the holdout Kingdom of Judah was gone.

And what of Jeremiah? The prophet's long life was a ribbon which uncoiled itself from a large spool, and that ribbon never changed its color. From the beginning to his latter days it was red, for Jeremiah's story was told in the red color of blood. Shortly before his capture the hunted and haunted Zedeiah summoned Jeremiah and inquired of the prophet whether he had heard word from God. Zedeiah's reaction was consistent with that of his predecessor Jehoiakim when he was informed by Jeremiah that Zedediah would be captured and taken to Babylonian imprisonment. Jeremiah was cast into prison and furnished the traditional diet of bread (one piece per day) and water until the supply of bread was exhausted. He was then lowered into a dark, dank cistern where lay no water but only mire, sludge and filth where he was compelled to lay Jeremiah, now an old man, most certainly faced death until saved through the intervention of God and his employment of an Ethiopian named Ebed-melech.

As deep as was the cistern into which the elderly prophet Jeremiah was cloistered, far deeper still were the reservoirs of patience. Not all Jews had been killed and not all have been transported into Babylonian captivity. A remnant remained and to them God renews the old, old promise that if you will follow Me, I will be your God, living under the wings of my love, patience and protection. The Lord Himself was faced with another old, old story. His rejection by the people. A remnant of the Jewish people seek safety and asylum and believe that it is not to be found in what remains of Judah. They decided then to make the long sojourn to Egypt, the other great power, in hopes that they can live under Pharaoh's, not God's protection, and assimilate into Egyptian society and culture. They even took Jeremiah with them, and they all faded from the pages of the Bible.

So, the centuries' story of God's patience with the Hebrew people came and went. It started with Moses's leading the Hebrews away from Pharaoh, Egyptian captivity and Egyptian patience. this epoch of their history now concludes with what is left of them voluntarily returning to Egypt and taking God's anointed, Jeremiah, with them. Sadly, the circle has now been completed. Our last recorded prophecies of Jeremiah find the old man still extolling the patience of God even in the face of the Jews' having turned to the worship of the goddess Ishtar while in Egypt. He foretold that this small remnant would soon die in Egyptian obscurity, as they did. A cloud of ignorance also envelopes the last days of Jeremiah, for the Old Testament provides no further record of his life or death.

Traditional beliefs proffer the explanation that Jeremiah was eventually stoned to death. Although no proof exists it is a reasonable conjecture given the consistent mistreatment which was meted out to him during his life. This was a lifetime sacrificed to as a rigorous a service to God that has ever been required of any man or woman, not excluding apostles. He was rejected by his family, subject to public humiliation, placed in stocks, repeatedly flogged, left in a pit to dies and eventually stoned to death. The weeping prophet, though, wept not for himself but for his country. Accuracy requires any observer to record that Jeremiah was with the possible exception of Isaiah, the most ineffective prophet ever chosen by God. For all he said, taught, preached, cajoled and begged to both kings and commoners he might as well have been blowing his words into the wind. The man died, but his reputation grew and must have grown to epic proportions. Over six hundred years later Jews was walking among stone pagan idols along the coast of Caesarea Philippi when he turned and asked His apostles "Whom do man say that I the Son of man am?" Before Peter gave the answer that recognized Him as the foundation of the Church. They replied that some consider you Lord as the coming again of ...Jeremiah.

Chapter 12

MALACHI – BACK HOME AGAIN

As God regretfully knew and as was prophesied several times over a span of centuries a remnant but only a remnant of Jews would survive the maelstrom of difficulties, defeats and horrors that the "Chosen People" had suffered. The northern kingdom of Israel was a faded memory, with most of its inhabitants taken by the Assyrians, and those not killed had been absorbed and assimilated losing all Jewish identity. To many historically they became the "lost Tribes" of Israel, although more accurately it would be stated that they were the tribes which committed national and cultural suicide. Now it was Judah's turn, but as with all histories we cannot force similarities. Judah was similar to Israel, but even in the fabric of uniformity wrinkles of distinction were noticed.

Although the land divided into two countries with two separate ruling families it must not be forgotten that legitimacy still rested with the crowned monarchs of Judah, for they were the successors to David. Moreover, while Judah could call a lengthy roll call of bad, even hellish, kings, it was not a nation bereft of great leadership at times, mostly during the reigns of Kings Hezekiah and Josiah. Israel had nothing but horrors in its rulers, none of whom had more, than at best, only a passing acknowledgement of God. Further, the northern Kingdom was borne in rebellion and never shook what was seemingly an endemic tendency to disobedience and idolatry. Judah had its moments, but moments they were, when it showed at least impulses to piety and disobedience. Yet all of this for both nations was now in the past. With Israel's passing into historical oblivion it was now Judah's turn.

The mass of Judah's population suffered and absorbed a series of Babylonian invasions, and this same mass was forcibly marched north and eastward to Babylon, there to serve as captives. The majority never returned to their ancient homeland along the eastern Mediterranean, and like their northern kin intermarried and were assimilated by the Gentiles of Babylon. To fully comprehend the period of Jewish history a brief examination of Babylon and the masters of the Jews, the Babylonians must be undertaken. Babylon itself occupied a region somewhat correspondent to modern Iraq, but it was an expansive power, continually pushing its borders in all directions. At the time of Judah's conquest, it was one of three great powers in this region of the world, the two others being Egypt to the West and the great Persian Empire to the east. The name of Babylon was well known and feared in antiquity, but unlike many others which have been forgotten by all but anthropologists and scholars of historical minutia it is a name that has resounded through the ages.

It would be needlessly tedious and repetitious to speak of the brutalities and even bestial behavior of the Babylonians for it would sound all too familiar. The ancient would was a protracted scene of brutality, and Babylon could stand in the fore with any of the old world's powers. Where Babylon "rose" above the others is its reputation for luxury, worldliness, love of beautiful homes and gardens and the sheer sordidness and immorality of many to its people, especially its upper classes. Into the twenty-first century Babylon has sustained its name and fame and to those familiar with the ancient world it remains a symbol of unbridled luxury and hedonism. It was a metaphorical title given to Rome by the apostle John when he penned Revelation, the Bible's final book, and described the Rome which persecuted Christians as a "harlot" or "whore drunken with the blood of the saints." Yet it remained powerful for some time and it had under its thumb Judah. Further, Babylon was ruled by one of ancient history's most striking figures, the enigmatic King Nebuchadnezzar, who was many things but certainly no fool. He selected from Judah's captive youth four young men, specifically chosen for their background, fine looks and intelligence, four young Jews who for once amply rewarded God's patience. They are known to us by the names Daniel, Shadrach, Meshach and Abednego. their stories have been spread since the days of the Old Testament and are not necessarily relevant to this work's theme – except – in one very important manner. Their dignity, adherence to moral principles and spirit of self-sacrifice for once rewarded God's patience. They were exemplary individuals and leaders, and their conduct and character was noted by Nebuchadnezzar. The King, a pagan to the core, nonetheless had deep respect for such men, Jewish or not, and he considered their God a force to be respected. As with all kings, though, he passed from the scene and was succeeded by his son Belshazzar. Belshazzar was every inch the idol worshipper as was his father, but he totally lacked his predecessor's wisdom and respect for the God of the Jews. In a banquet party scene brilliantly described in the scriptures the King decided that it would be amusing to drink wine from the holy vessels which had been pilfered from the temple in Jerusalem. In a tableau that surpasses the most macabre modern movie horror film while the King and his hordes were indulging in exuberant drinking and brazenly committing a sacrilege, suddenly a disembodied hand appeared and began writing on the wall the words "Mene, mene, tekel, upharsin" translated into our English as "You have been weighed in the balances and found wanting." Belshazzar's attention was diverted from his drink to the handwriting on the wall and was so terrified that

"...the joints of his loins were loosed, and his knees smote one against another."

That very night the Persian army, which had been besieging Babylonia, broke through and Babylon was finished as a power, being subsumed by the Persian Empire. The fascinating tale is evidence that God's patience with those who are not His children is not extended as generously as it is with His own.

Now, the Jews were under the rule of the mammoth and magnificent Persian Empire composed of 127 provinces stretching from the sub-continent of India to the sub-Saharan African nation of Ethiopia. For once, though, Judah was ruled by an empire that was not quite as exacting and despotic as the other powers who had sought to crush Judah. In fact, may Jews occupied positions of importance in the Persian government, particularly Mordechai, the uncle of a beautiful young Jewish girl named Esther, who had been espoused to the great emperor himself, Ahasuerus (known in western history as Xerxes). Again, as with Daniel and his companions the retelling of the story of Mordechai and Esther is not here compelled, other than to exclaim that both joined the ranks of Daniel and associates as moral exemplars, truly rewarding, at least in part, God's patience.

It has been noted that not all the Jews of Judah were taken to Babylonian captivity in a rush, there having gradually been removed in successive waves of humanity and settled in the Babylonian (later Persian) Empire. Neither did they return to Judah in a large group, but slowly most of the remaining Jews returned to Judah, which remained a portion of the Persian Empire. Late in the 500's B.C., after seventy years of cruel captivity the return was essentially completed, with two outstanding leaders having stepped forward, Ezra and Nehemiah. Ezra was a scribe, highly trained in the Law of Moses and Nehemiah, a somewhat more flamboyant figure, was on the staff of the Persian King Artaxerxes I, serving as the royal cupbearer. Both separately and together these men encouraged the repopulation of Jerusalem and the reconstruction of the Temple which the Babylonians had destroyed. It was under Nehemiah, possessing a royal commission that the Jews had rebuilt the temple, despite facing ferocious opposition of other Persian governors and even some of the Jews themselves.

After several generations and endless tragedies and national catastrophes the Jews were back in Judah and Jerusalem was re-established as the capital and religious center of the nation. The people, so long out of any sort of synchronization with the revealed religion of Sinai had to be retaught and both Ezra and Nehemiah, but especially Ezra took the lead in solidifying Judaism as the religion of the people. Ezra emphasized three points in his teaching, the first being obvious, that is to adhere to the Law of Moses. Secondly, the keeping of the Sabbath, so long abandoned by most of the Jews was firmly taught, and the third factor being a strong caveat against their intermarrying with the heathen Gentiles. All these matters were easily taught, easily heard and most importantly easily ignored. It was the old Judah yet. More importantly and quite pertinently it was the same God.

In this reconstituted Jewish society in the fifth century B.C. a new prophet appeared, a man of whom we literally know only two things. His name was Malachi, meaning "the messenger" and he was the author of a short four-chapter book, the final book in the compilation of the books of most Old Testament. He really made no prophecy to any specific individual, but rather one not just to the Jewish nation but also to the entire world. Written some 2,500 years ago its subject matter and the problems it addresses bear a striking resemblance to modern society. Not modern society alone, though, but to ancient Jewish society for it takes but little time for this apostate people to relapse into the same attitude and practices of the past. Yet, for now, though, we will see that God's patience does not break, for time has moved steadily along its continuum and the Lord is closer to fulfilling His promises and plans.

So, the Jewish remnant is back, and they are once again receiving prophecy. Earthly names and faces have changed, but the same God remains. Malachi commences his prophecy with a simple statement that God still loves them and then provides a brief history of protective hand He has always extended over Judah and how the enemies of His people are ultimately all destroyed. Malachi, though, surely aware that he was commissioned to write only a brief book of prophecy gets right to the few sharp, salient points he intends to make. He initially addresses the problems of a particular group, or perhaps more accurately stated "caste" of persons, who have proven extremely problematic since the days of Aaron, the original priest under Judaism, and that of course is the priesthood itself.

Introducing this subject in Malachi's day let it be generally stated that the priesthood, the designated spiritual leaders of the people, had resumed and were seemingly perfecting many of their historical habits of indifference, indolence and insincerity. The Divine Eye easily captured this in His field of vision and knowledge, and the disappointment of a patient God indeed was deep. To recall all the corrupt priests of the Old Testament and the mockery that so many attempted to make of religion would indeed be tedious. Nevertheless, in general their history was blotted and sordid and how painful and enraging it must have been to the Lord to witness this new group of post-exilic priest walking in the footsteps of yore. The curious will now query, "What was it that the priests were doing that was so bad?" These men, all from the ancient tribe of Levi, had been set apart by the certain statements of God, directed to wear special clothing to signify recognition and respect as the spiritual guides and leaders of God's people. They had failed, not just fallen short, but failed abysmally, intentionally and in such blasphemous and sacrilegious ways that the almost infinite patience of God had reached what we might call "terminal velocity." The priests' performance resulted in some of the Bible's harshest language and in a wording, which is shocking to both believer and non-believer.

Under the Levitical Law the priests were given the duties both substantive and ceremonial, of offering the required animal sacrifices to God. The Mosaical Law specifically established that only the very best specimens were to be offered to God. Obviously, the sacrifice of a defective or diseased animal was no sacrifice at all. the people and especially the priests, chose the latter course, openly disdaining the Law and the express wishes and instructions of God. Through Malachi's words God excoriated the priests and assured them that any of their blessings and privileges would be turned to curses. The, in words that still provide a jolt to the reader:

"I will corrupt your seed, and spread dung upon your faces, even the dung of your solemn feasts;

and one shall take you away with it."

The term "dung" is not a common in modern speech, but its meaning and the disgust, disdain and shock which the word picture of this language presents still shakes us. Likely one would not be incorrect if he surmised that God's reservoirs of patience with the priesthood, deep though they were, had been drained to the last few drops of His tolerance. As bad as they had become, though, God knew that the worst from this class was yet to be realized, and would not be fully revealed until the time of His son when their perfidy and wretchedness would be on full display in the conspiracy to crucify Christ, led by the High Priest himself, Caiaphas.

God knew that His ordained priesthood was simply "going through the motions," a practice which has always been anathema to Him. So disgusted was He that He directed that the doors of the temple be closed, and no more services be held, the modern

Christian equivalent being closing the Church. It could all be traced to the priests.

Only an inveterate atheist and/or skeptic would seriously allege that all priests, ministers, members of the clergy, etc., have always been and still are hopelessly corrupt. This willfully ignores too much Biblical and historical evidence of too many men whose lives were selflessly devoted to the service of God and humanity, many of whom became martyrs. The atheist rejoices in the bad character of any Christian but especially that of the clergy, but the same clerical vices bring embarrassment and dismay to the Christian. An historical aside may be pursued for a short distance when it is averred that the clerical class has historically and consistently tried the patience of God. The early apostasy of the church revealed the priests, the bishops and others of various nomenclature bringing the church low. The Protestant Reformation of the 1400's and 1500's was partially engendered by an almost endemic corruption of the Roman Catholic hierarchy, a corruption which, especially in recent times, the Catholic clergy has grudgingly admitted. As for the Reformation remarkable and morally sound men such as William Tyndale and Martin Luther were in the forefront of change and correction, but the Reformation itself produced a plentiful share of place-seekers and self-servers in its clerisy. More modern times have had to endure an almost endless parade of charlatans, spiritual "carnival barkers" and frauds who become hedonistic multi-millionaires as self-proclaimed servants and yes, even prophets, of God. How His patience must be stretched to its limits, but we see from both Testaments and here from Malachi there is "nothing new under the sun."

Neither did the mass of the people escape the indignation of the prophet as Malachi focused on two issues especially which were exhausting God's patience. The Law of God had always prescribed that God's people tithe of their earnings as a means of sacrifice and glorification of Him. Yet these Israelites, the remnant who had been spared from the various holocausts of the Old Testament times were loathe and deeply reluctant to part with any property to God. God saw in the decline of giving and the giving pattern which had been established by the people dismal signs of the wholesale materialism which can so easily grasp and destroy any society. Sacrifice and sacrificial giving are consistently huge issues with God as we are reminded that the one instance in the Gospels where Christ displays His temper was in the cleansing of the temple, where the moneychangers and some priests have putrefied giving itself into an act of degeneracy.

As bad as these matters were, though, perhaps it was a practice which the Jewish people increasingly had adopted of which God disapproved and in which He saw the greatest peril for the Jews. Malachi wrote at some length on the increasingly common Jewish practice of intermarriage with the pagan Gentiles. Neither the marriage nor the practice dwelled in any sort of sterile isolation. Malachi knew that the marriage of Israelite men to pagan women often followed the divorce of an Israelite wife, thus destroying a marriage which God had blessed. With even longer-range consequences God saw that the marriage to the Gentile most often led the Jew into Gentile heathenism with its catastrophic effects. Certainly, no contention can be made that the Gentile and his/her soul was any less valued than the Jew, but rather God's prohibition was centered on the historical reality that this practice could easily lead the nation into apostasy and paganism, as had so often happened before. Whether it was the message of Malachi, a reawakening of religious devotion or just a factor in the historical sweep of events for once things went right in Judah, and right upon an issue of huge proportions. After the return from Babylonian captivity the sins of the Jewish nation were as scarlet, and the New Testament, especially the Gospels, reveals the hardness of hearts and of the society at large. The one transgression of which they no longer partook was that of idolatry. To this degree the seventy years of exile had chastened the Jewish nation, and they were ready to acknowledge God as the one true God. Unfortunately, they continued to fall short in any many areas and in many fashions their hearts were hardened, but no longer did they turn their faces to the gods of Egypt, Babylon nor to Baal and Moloch. God's patience tested to a degree and a depth that proved He was Divine, was herein rewarded.

Now, the direct voice of God as He spoke through the prophets falls silent for some four hundred years. The works of the Jews changes not by gradualism but by political, military and cultural earthquakes, Judah is buffeted, persecuted, humiliated but finally not only survives an attempted holocaust in the second century B.C. but triumphs and finds unity and pride, perhaps too much pride, in being Jews, the chosen People of God. But before the prophetic voice from Heaven lapses into silence Malachi utters one final prophecy:

> "Behold, I will send you Elijah the prophet before the coming of the great and dreadful day of the Lord."

Chapter 13

JOHN THE BAPTIST – ODE TO JOY

*T*he world changed. From the turning of the final page of the final book of the Old Testament, Malachi, to the opening page of the New Testament in the Gospel of Matthew some four hundred years elapse. The world, especially that of the Bible, is so altered by the tides of human history that in any sense it becomes almost unrecognizable from what went before. The primary stage, though, on which the Bible's events are recorded remains the same, and in point of fact actually narrows during the time of the Gospel events of which we shall speak. Although the land, the geography, and the terrain are identical the spotlight is no longer on that land which at various states was Israel, Israel and Judah, and finally Judah alone. Now, same though it may be, it is called Judea. Therein lies a tale, a story not told in the narrative pages of either Testament but from other sources and its grasp and understanding is requisite to our understanding of the times into which the prophesized Elijah would be borne.

Malachi, our final Old Testament prophet recorded in circa 400 B.C. that the captive and exiled Jews had made the trek from Babylonian and later Persian captivity and had resettled in the ancient homeland of Judah. The small land was still under the sovereignty of the Persians, although because of the light hand of Persian rule it was certainly not slavery. In many respects Judah was independent and most importantly they were free to pursue their religion without persecution and interference. Yet, Persia itself had seen better days, and it had seriously weakened and shown its limitations by the previous century's wars with the Greeks, which gave history the names of battles still studied, Thermopylae, Marathon, Salamis and Plataea. It regained a massive land power, though, and remained an attractive prize tempting the most adventurous of conquerors. The prize and such a man found each other. In the West the Greek civilization had begun its rise two centuries before, and bursting forth from this small rocky terrain in southeastern Europe came a flood of scientific, artistic and literary development rarely, if ever, equaled by any civilization. The spread of this Greek (or more commonly then "Hellenic" culture) upended ancient customs, traditions, gods and religions, and the self-ordained hybrid flower of the Greeks, a young Macedonian king styled Alexander the Great crossed into Asia and for the next twelve years made conquest of everything in sight, even mighty Persia, and more directly to our interest Judah. Alexander, though, died at the age of 32, and soon his great empire was divided into three separate empires ruled by the separate dynasties. Eventually the Jews fell under the rule of the Seleucids, a Greco-Syrian power, which for a century or more held sway in much of the Biblical world. The crown in this dynastic succession eventually fell onto the head of a man named Antiochus Epiphanes IV, who desired greater reign and glory than his inherited empire provided. By the time of his reign in the 170's B.C. a greater power than had ever been seen on this earth was rising in the west on the Italian Peninsula on the Tiber River, Rome. The ego and greed of Antiochus was great, and he built an army which he hoped ready to slake his thirst for conquest, even if it meant challenging Rome itself. But first he had to overcome a fateful problem in his own domain.

Hellenism had spread east and west, Greek culture, language and thinking, and it was a unifying force among peoples and nations. All cultures which Hellenism touched became Greek in thinking and religion, all that is save one – Judah. The Jews resisted this cultural absorption which Antiochus saw as an act of brazen defiance and a weakening of his political and military power. He thus initiated an early Holocaust, as thorough and brutal, as anything practiced by the Nazis. Tens of thousands of Jews were mercilessly slaughtered, and the end of the Chosen People was seemingly at hand.

From the most overlooked and unusual sources often comes the greatest stories. In 167 B.C. a quiet, humble elderly priest named Mattathias, after a confrontation with the officials of Antiochus, called together his five sons and told them that the end of Judah and God's Promise to Abraham was within sight, and the destruction of the Jewish people and God's plans was within vision. If the Jews were to survive, he exclaimed, his sons must lead the war for survival. The middle some, Judas Maccabees, took the lead and led the Jewish Revolt, a war of survival and of independence from the Seleucids. His brothers joined as leaders, and after several years of battles thrillingly told in the Apocrypha the Jews won, retained their freedom and developed a pride in being Jews, a pride that they had rarely demonstrated. Perhaps too much pride.

A soul and nation destroying burden of the Jews of the Old Testament was that they wanted above all else to be like other nations, and had no sensitivity or understanding of the special role given the Jewish people. Now, the Jews were proud, rightly proud it must be added, of their heritage and special role as God's Chosen People, the people of the ancient covenant with Abraham. Gentiles and their ways began to be reviled as dogs and almost sub-human, and the priestly caste grew in power and influence. These were the days of the burgeoning growth of religious sects, most prominently the Pharisees and Sadducees of New Testament notoriety. This trend continued unabated even with the coming of the Romans in 63 B.C., when now once again Judah lost its freedom. Now, though, it was no longer Judah, but rather Judea, the "Land of the Jews" to the Romans, The Romans with their military prowess and superb organizational skills ruled strictly but in general left the Jews to their own religion (a faith which baffled the Romans) and affairs continued at peace, though at times a restless and tense peace, for several decades to follow.

Late in the reign of King Herod the Great, a part Jewish confidante of the Romans and a man possessed of both extraordinary political skills and extraordinarily low morals, an elderly and righteous Jewish priest named Zacharias was informed by an angel that his wife Elisabeth would give birth to a son, the Elijah of Malachi's prophecy and so it happened. Though not named Elijah the boy named John grew into a young man with a strong resemblance to the great prophet of old. John's character, dress and to an extent his impact was quite similar to the great prophet of old; however, his coming and his message were fashioned by God in an entirely different manner. Whereas Elijah makes a sudden appearance in 800's B.C. Israel, unannounced, unprophesied and without any specified pedigree John the Baptist is the mirror opposite.

His parents and lineage is fully detailed and John stands in a singular position as the only prophet whose coming is itself prophesied. Many of the prophets on whom we have shined the light of study were chosen suddenly (or at least suddenly to the people, but perhaps not to God), but John's coming had been announced over seven centuries before its actual realization. The great prophet Isaiah first proclaimed that before the coming of the Lord would be:

> "(a) voice crying in the wilderness, Prepare ye the
> way of the Lord, make straight in the desert a high-
> way for our God."

The benedictory prophetic writer in the Old Testament, Malachi, proclaimed that this person "...shall prepare the way before me, and the Lord, whom ye seek, shall suddenly come to His temple." Before we ponder and study the coming of the Lord let us do as He apparently meant and examine this last prophet.

Who was this prophet, the man with the odd appellation of John "the Baptist?" How did he appear to people and what was His message? For understandable reasons the middle of these three questions has been the one capturing so much attention from John's time to our current age. Remarkably, except for what might be termed glancing references the New Testament offers no physical description of any man or woman. Unlike in the Old no woman is ever described as beautiful and desirable, and similarly no man is termed either strong or handsome. The closest the Testament comes to a description is that of John the Baptist, and it is certainly arresting of anyone's attention. One of the greatest understatements that could be uttered is that John lived a rough rustic life. The Gospels inform us that he lived in the wilderness and dressed in garments made of camel's hair and a leather belt. His diet was one which likely would be acceptable to the most extreme environmentalist, nutritionist or naturalist for he sustained himself on locusts and wild honey. To history and likely to most of his contemporaries he is a "wild man," living at a primitive level, isolated from others and vehemently condemning any and all who displease him. The description of his appearance is, in fact, remarkably similar to Elijah's, a name which was utilized as descriptive of John. While his appearance and lifestyle indeed denote a rough-hewn man, was John the Baptist an ancient crazy man? To answer that inquiry factors more substantial than physical appearance and perception must be examined.

For a man who supposedly lived in isolation John had little difficulty in drawing multitudes to hear his message and more important great numbers of obedient hearers and even some followers, including many of the apostles themselves. The people gathered in hordes, notably at the Jordan River to hear his prophecy, and many obeyed his call for baptism unto repentance by being immersed in the Jordan itself. John's message has frequently been described by both detractors and admirers as "harsh" but that is improper and basically even incorrect. As was Elijah's challenge to Ahab and Jezebel, John's message was stark, unvarnished and likely meant to be heavy on shock value, as was his appearance. Who could deny the trepidation and amazement with which multitudes heard phrases such as:

> "O generation of vipers, who hath warned you to flee from the wrath to come."

or

> "...now the axe is laid unto the trees: every tree therefore which bringeth not forth good fruit is hewn down, and cast into the fire."

Phraseology which addresses the audience as effectively a "bunch of snakes" that will be going to hell customarily adds little to the speaker's popularity. Yet, we shall see that the prophet's message was far removed from the fire and wrath which this suggests. John knew, as did the Prophesied One who followed even more, that the Jews' religion had become a tangled web of every law, rules and regulations, its primary purpose being the scrupulous and meticulous observance of the outward forms of faith (or at least of their own traditions) while their hearts were actually far from God. It had become a maze, a labyrinth of man-made rules and its leaders and practitioners as vile to God as was the corrupt priesthood of the Old

Testament. The day was at hand, said John when the hearts of all would be revealed, and the times of God's patience exhausted.

Was this all the great prophet had to proclaim? Harsh denunciations, scathing rebukes and devastating criticisms, none of which could really bind the heart of a man or woman to any belief or person. Actually, not at all, for much of John's teaching was very similar to what the Old Testament prophets had been issuing for generations, even centuries. John's teaching, though, was more direct, more situation specific and far more personal than anything heard before. He addressed individuals and groups with living admonitions on just exactly how their lives could be improved and more pleasing to God. For example, startling as it may seem to us who have been conditioned to think of professional soldiers, especially those of the ancient Romans, as licentious brutes, some were in attendance when John spoke. They had no reticence when they asked him "What shall we do?" His response then was as shocking and instructive as it remains today:

> "Do violence to no man, neither accuse any falsely;
> and be content with your wages."

The prophet's few words encompass acres of ground, and only a blinkered-eyed literalist would apply them to soldiers only. Treat all justly and with respect, and do not abuse your authority. But the rub lies in the encouragement of monetary contentment. Doubtless, neither these soldiers nor any person before or since has been condemned for seeking to better the situation with improved employment. The attitude that seems to be condemned is prolonged discontent and what in another place is determined to be "murmuring and disputing."

To another group, even more hated and more onerous to the populace, he spoke plainly. These were the publicans, the tax collecting clique, hated by most as preying vultures upon the Jewish people.

They were simply told to "...exact no more than that which is appointed you." In everyday terms, deal honestly, again a lesson for all for all ages, a strong facet and pillar of what later came to be known as the Golden Rule. But to everyone in the audience he offered familiar words:

> "He that hath two coats, let him impart to him that
> hath none; he that hath meat, let him do likewise."

Was John teaching a communist or even a socialist economic system to us? No, for God's word from His prophets and apostles in the Bible itself has only a small, even tangential interest in such matters as economic systems. What John does once again is provide the answer to the question asked thousands of years earlier of "Am I my brother's keeper." Every word, every action, every decree, commandment or even Biblical nuance answers the question with a resounding "Yes." How much of the world's history, though, is a sad chronicle of the disregard for this simple principle.

As for moral teaching in general the few days allotted John the Baptist really add nothing to the directive of either the Old or New Testaments. Nothing he said was really new and had been known by all worshippers for millennia, even before Moses and the codification of the Law. The element, which John added and even two thousand years is felt from his words is a sense, a dire sense of urgency, for as he proclaimed "(T)he kingdom of heaven is at hand." Great prophets and great men such as Elijah and Elisha spoke to the moral dilemmas of the day and concentrated on redirecting the paths of the straying Israelites. The prophet Isaiah for decades spoke of matters the fulfillment of which would occur over seven centuries later, and the estimable Jeremiah and others like him mainly contended with the moral degradation into which kings and their kingdoms had fallen. It was to John, this strange man, dressing strangely and seeming to live in the isolation of the wilderness who was assigned the task of not merely prophecy but of the proclamation of the "present" rather than 'future" events.

John the Baptist is deserving and his mission demanding of a closer scrutiny of just how wild and isolated a man he was. For a wild man John was astonishingly approachable and a person who did not intimidate. He and his messages were magnetic to multitudes, and all strata of society seemed to have no reluctance in conversing and questioning him as to his teachings on any issues. Publicans, soldiers, the great populace and as we shall see even kings carried no reluctance into their contacts with him. As for isolation he was a man of remarkable awareness and astuteness to the events and issues of the day and the trends of public opinion. John's wilderness home was no preclusion to his having a keen and seemingly more than superficial understanding of the day's political situation. Herod Antipas was then king over much of the territory long ruled by his father Herod the Great. Antipas inherited not only his father's kingly power but his moral fabric as well. He was what may now be termed a social adulterer and was married to a woman named Herodias, neither being their first marriage and Herodias being the former wife of the brother Herod Agrippa. John preached against this adultery at the pinnacle of political power, was cast into prison primarily at the insistence of Herodias. Nonetheless, while confined, he made the acquaintance of Herod Antipas, who enjoyed his discussions with the strange holy prophet and apparently developed a sincere respect for him, a respect not shared by his comely wife, Herodias. In one of history's most told and famous stories, through the machinations of Herodias, the seductive feminine charms of her daughter Salome and the sheer stupidity and weakness of Herod Antipas, John the Baptist was murdered.

A young man and a young prophet John the Baptist left this world of mortality while in his early thirties. His delivery was shocking and his messages truly and deeply meaningful, but beyond that was his life as a prophet truly different than that of the great men before him. While in no way diminishing the stature of those men, many of whom were martyred and were his predecessors the answer to this question is yes, John the Baptist was different.

The immediacy of his message and the lasting depth of his moral teaching are with us yet. For a very brief time John the Baptist was the religious celebrity of Judea, a nation which to outsiders, especially appeared to be drunk with religion and religious teaching. In his position, many men (and history has not been hesitant to identify and publicize them) have succumbed to the lure of celebrity, blunted their moral teachings and themselves become hypocrites. Not so with John the Baptist. Except for the one who followed John he showed as much true humility as any man in the Bible, perhaps ever. He knew that if his own disciples would be patient one was coming "...the latchet of whose shoes I am not worthy to unloose." John was aware as great as was his role that he was a supporting player and their patience should abide in place just a bit longer. He was quite content to be the "friend of the bridegroom" at the great wedding and marriage about to come. Not only was John the Baptist content with his station and role he foresaw and desired its diminishment, and in words of modesty and self-effacement that have never been surpassed he exclaimed that: "He must increase, but I must decrease."

The patience of God had endured for ages, and in one of its forms it has been easy to view but hard to contemplate. How often people's conduct and contempt for Him merited His punishment, yet the Lord invariably stayed His hand, and His patience served His people time after endless time. He chose to abide the childishness of His people, former slaves, when they were led from Egypt, and He endured for decades, generations and even centuries the colossally blatant disregard the people had for Him, their Creator. Moreover, God's likely desire for destruction withstood and held firm during the trying and despairing years of Ahab and Jezebel. The patience of the Lord of Hosts finally lapsed with Israel and then Judah, but yet with the latter just as a remnant of the people remain so likewise did a remnant of God's patience. When they returned, chastened from Babylonian and then Persian captivity, He remained their God.

Hopefully, this type of God's patience has been thoroughly chronicled, but another facet of patience has been overlooked. It is the patience of anticipation, a patience in which John the Baptist was inextricably involved. this is that patience which a person feels when he anticipates the reaction of one whom he loves is about to receive a gift. It has never been better or more succinctly expressed in the phrase "I cannot wait to give this to you." For the giver senses and believes that the gift will be greater, perhaps immensely greater than anything he could contemplate. At that moment when the gift is actually made and the recognition, perhaps joy, perhaps even ecstasy, is seen on the face and in the reaction of the recipient, the donor realizes the worth and glory of his own patience. Likely in this world it was most deeply experienced that day when John the Baptist, the greatest of all prophets, was teaching and turned to see his own kinsman, with a proud and triumphant proclamation announced: "Behold the Lamb of God, which taketh away the sin of the world."

CONCLUSION

Patience is not an element itself, but rather it is a complex compound composed of numerous elements, many of which are burdened with essentially unpleasant connotations. The word patience is rarely, if ever, employed with persons, ideas or events that are found to be enjoyable. The sentence 'I patiently endured a superlative, delicious dinner" is not to be simply because it is a ridiculous oxymoron, a gross contradiction in terms. Rather, individuals on a daily basis enlist the word patience and its synonyms to describe a dietary regime which they are having to endure. We are not required to examine any non-Biblical source to discover the term which the Bible repeatedly uses as descriptive of patience and one which is almost self-descriptive and self-defining, and that, of course is "longsuffering." No one ever speaks of their pleasant enjoyment of suffering of enduring something for a protracted period of time. The Bible clearly demonstrates to us that measured by the timekeeping of the world no one could ever hope to equal its Creator for longsuffering.

The longsuffering of God is measured not in days, hours and minutes but rather in years, centuries and millennia. We recall His patient suffering with the Hebrews' enslavement for centuries, which suffering must have intensified after He finally secured their emancipation. Beginning with Moses and the dawn of the Prophetic Age the prophet's own mortal and finitely limited patience was taxed to its limits, as men such as Moses, Samuel, Elijah, Elisha, Isaiah and Jeremiah suffered in their own lives, and the sufferings were for a "long" time. As much as any of the humanity these men understood or came to understand real patience. Yet longsuffering is composed of at least two elemental factors, the "long" and the "suffering". It is more than just waiting on a person or a situation to improve, and the wait taking a considerable period of time. It is also the suffering, the pain, which must be endured, and the bible is a veritable compendium of paid, most of its God's. He endured the pain, the most bitter disappointments, when the freed Hebrews continually rebelled, complained and displayed their deepest ingratitude towards Him. How great must God's suffering have been when He witnessed that by the reign of King Ahab, the northern Kingdom of Israel had so degraded itself that His handful of worshippers which remained were at constant risk of their lives. The pain of seeing messengers of the caliber of men such as Isaiah and Jeremiah being rejected must have tested the Divine mettle any further. The prophets were ignored, ridiculed and in some cases even murdered, and yet God's plan for the redemption of Israel and of humanity itself remained.

A huge portion of the virtue of patience is simply waiting, and who, especially in the modern society in which we live, enjoys waiting? God measures time differently than do we, but still it is an element of His patience. All mankind realizes that a major component of "patiently waiting" is a hope, the hope that a situation will improve, or a problem will be solved. Therein lies the torment, the acid that eats away at the hopes of a person who tries to be patient, who is willing to wait and yet wonders whether the wait, the patience will be all awarded. Likewise, also therein lies an astonishing wonder of God in that He demonstrates and has always evidenced patience when He in His omniscience knew that His hopes and desires would not be rewarded. He knew, not supposed, not wondered, not guessed, but knew that in the main Israel, Judah and His Chosen People, the Jews, would reject Him and His prophets. His patience was retained, though, for God had far greater goals which He intended to fulfill.

Let us pose now the central, the decisive and the most important question. Was it worth it? Was God's endlessly enduring patience worth it for Himself? Was and is it worth it, or any sense merited, to mankind, we the time worn recipients of God's endless patience? If we demonstrate patience, as some, though not many of the Jews managed, will there be a reward, a sufficient reward for our patience?

Let us for a moment focus our inquiry on the initial question of whether God's patience has been or perhaps will be rewarded. God's satisfaction and rewards are determined by God alone. All we know of His thinking is determined by what He has revealed to us, told us and in some manner demonstrated to us. We are denied full knowledge of His mind, for among His own good reasons, none of us could really grasp all His thinking. He spoke with Divine eloquence through His prophet Isaiah when He stated "(M)y ways are higher than your ways, and My thoughts than your thoughts."

Yet it is not fully speculative, however, when we ponder His thinking and His emotions based upon what He tells us and has had demonstrated to mankind. Simply stated the fulfillment of all Biblical prophecies and the full glorious revelation of God's intentions came in the person of His Son, Jesus Christ. God's first reward and His prize for His own patience is His being able to share the magnificence of His Son with all humanity.

When we left the last and greatest of the prophets, John the Baptist, upon seeing his own cousin, Jesus son of Joseph and Mary approaching, realized that the days of wailing were over and excitedly exclaimed "Behold the Lamb of God." Following the baptism of Jesus by John the Holy Spirit, in the bodily form of a dove descended upon Jesus and a heavenly voice proclaimed "Thou art my beloved Son; in thee I am well pleased."

All fathers and mothers, except the neglectful, the cynical and the embittered are proud of their children and generally wish the world to be aware of what they have produced. A good parent, within the limits of propriety and modesty, welcomes all opportunities to "show off" a son or daughter and should not necessarily be reticent in demonstrating a rightful pride in their offspring. Such emotions are not self-generated by humans, and if have them it is because they were placed within us by our Heavenly Father, who first possessed them. Our children, though, however wonderful they may be, however beautiful, intelligent and well-spoken remain flawed humans, but regardless our pride in them is not diminished. Consider the Creator when at last He not only prophesied and spoke of His coming but was able to show to all the world how glorious was His Son. God's patience received a great reward.

How deep, how beautiful and how magnificent must the Father's thoughts have been when in part the world would now see and contemplate the beauty of His Son, a Son so radiantly beautiful that the scriptures require over one hundred twenty separate names simply to describe Him. The Prince of Peace, the Good Shepherd, the Master and on and on down a golden path of description they scribe, but maybe one among all others comes closest when He is entitled the Alpha and Omega, the beginning and the end, literally everything, the meaning of existence in the person of one man, the Son of Man. God now could and would demonstrate the purpose and the reward of hundreds and hundreds of years of patience in the form of just one man and how glorious He must have been and appeared. Only He did not. He appeared in physical form as an ordinary man with average looks and appearance, a common demeanor which itself had been long prophesied in the Old Testament. In fact, He was the least royalty and kingly of kings, borne in the most humble circumstances imaginable. Jesus, the Son of God, the "reward" for humanity's patience was reared in an ordinary family by two parents who lay claim to no earthly fame. He was raised in the non-descript village of Nazareth, in Galilee on the farthest edge of the Roman Empire, the center of the world. For his heritage and background, He could claim a backwater village in the contemptible province of Galilee in Judea, to many of the Romans the very ends of the earth, or at least the backend of the Empire.

The trade of this Messiah, the expected King, was that of carpentry, an important occupation, then and now, but one that is favored with little status and prestige. So, he had no particular pedigree, came from the most modest and humble background, had no particular formal education credentials and worked a "blue-collar" trade. This is what the people, in the first instance the Jews, were to accept as the prophetic reward for their patience? Underlying the four gospel accounts is the emotion, spoken at times and silent at others, of the people's disappointment with God. Surely this is not the Messiah, the Prophesied One, agreed the priestly caste, for he is not one of us. the multitudes rejected Him for various reasons, not least of which was that He was not a King in the mold of a David, who would lead them in ousting the Romans or that he really offered no real change in their daily, ordinary lives. As the scriptures foretold: "He came unto His own, and His own received Him not."

Despised and rejected of men He did not seem the stuff of legends, the fulfillment of anyone's desires, and He did not rouse the glory of a David, an Alexander or a Caesar. Underlying the very public hatred and rejection, though, was a discipleship from some, then and now, which doubtless gratified and rewarded God's patience even more than did any of the Old Testament faithful.

His true disciples then and His true disciples now grasp what the apostle meant when he described Him as one "...a bruised reed shall He not break." Those who awaited His coming understood His meaning when He admonished other eager disciples to "...let the little children come unto Me, for such is the Kingdom of God." The devoted Jew and now the devoted Christian sees the great patience of God and of the disciple, too, when he hears the words of the Savior:

> "Come unto me all ye that labor, and I will give you
> rest... For my yoke is easy and my burden is light."

The true loving disciple, even through years of labor, hardship and grief realizes through God's Word and through the words and example of His Son that all this is temporal, temporary, for hereafter life will alter in the twinkling of an eye and that the last shall be first and the first, last.

For as long as God has disciples His patience will be rewarded. That period is forever, as Christ expounded that no matter what evil came (and He knew it would) His church would stand for the very "... gates of hell will not prevail against it." God's patience is rewarded whenever the humblest approaches Him in prayer, whenever He sees His own doing unto others as they would have done unto them, and in all those moments of self-sacrifice, great and small, that His children willingly provide. Most of all, His patience is bountifully blessed when He sees anyone, anywhere and in any circumstance, who glorifies Him and His Son.

So, it was worth it for God, the agonizing centuries of rejection and rebellion, all of which culminated in the crucifixion of His Son on Calvary, and the daily crucifixion in which the mass of mankind rejects Him and holds Him in contempt? Christ often spoke of rewards, and in one instance at minimum He spoke of the least act, the smallest service being a reward to both the doer and God when He said:

> "Whosoever shall give to drink unto one of these
> little ones a cup of cold water only in the name of a
> disciple... he shall in no wise lose his reward."

Since God has provided so much indication, we do not consider ourselves presumptuous when we exclaim that yes, His patience has been rewarded.

God was proud of His Son and we might even say awkwardly that He gloried in His Son's glory. Jesus lived the life of perfect exemplary humility, but one day (which we denote as Palm Sunday) God was able to revel in the glory of His Son. As Jesus rode into Jerusalem on a donkey the multitudes placed palm leaves in his fore for Him to ride over as they hailed Him as "Blessed is the King of Israel." The ever-cynical negative Pharisees desired to rebuke the crowd for their tumult, but Jesus responded that such was God's desire to glorify Christ that if all remained silent even the stones in the road would cry in exultation. God indeed was rewarded in this moment.

The rewards for God's patience, though, cannot be measured in mass movements or in national trends or in the spiritual state of a religious or church hierarchy. Rather it is measured one by one, one person and one heart at a time. Whether and to an extent how far and deeply is God's patience is dependent upon the answer of each individual's heart to His Son's call. One of the clear messages from the scriptures is that God neither saves nor condemns souls enmasse, but rather makes His eternal determination based upon each individual's life.

This small work has centered on the immense patience which God has demonstrated through the ages and from which the world itself and His followers specifically have been the beneficiaries. What of our patience, though? Is not one of the prime Christian virtues' patience, a lesson demonstrated repeatedly and taught without ceasing in both Testaments? Contrary to the miasma of moral teaching offered in the world, in reality God expects us to do nothing without the promise of reward. Being patient and longsuffering is a prime virtue and one of the foundational stones of a Christian character. Impatience and true Christian character are not comfortable companions and with too much familiarity they will eventually sever each other's company. Yet, Christians as do those of the world expect a reward for their efforts. The expectation is often unspoken, and when verbalized "reward" is not always the word which is employed. Christ recognized and spoke of the expectations of His own detractors, many of which were key components of the religious establishment of that day. Of the ravishing desires of the scribes and Pharisees for continuous public praise, approval and exaltation he simply stated, "They have their reward," the obvious implication being that the reward for their lives was fleeting and temporal.

But of His own and to His own Christ spoke intimately of recompense for lives of labor, worry, even outright persecution and onerous demands on patience. No group has more exemplary or representative of this then the twelve apostles. His closest confidantes, and the men who shared much of His life for three years. What demands will be made upon you He explained, for your enemies will consider you lower than dirt, will hate you, torment you and eventually believe that when they kill you, they are doing God service. Demands will be placed on you which the non-believer could not withstand, and they will be continual, life-long, requiring the deepest reserves of patience. For this Christ gently, simply and firmly told them and all His disciples with words whose simplicity and sincerity heighten their impact that: "Great is your reward in Heaven."

How appropriate it is that patience, the Queen of Virtues, is rewarded by the King of Kings.

www.ingramcontent.com/pod-product-compliance
Lightning Source LLC
Chambersburg PA
CBHW060242050426
42448CB00009B/1557

* 9 7 8 1 6 3 3 5 7 1 9 7 6 *